REVISED EDITION

QUICKBOOKS

ONLINE

BEGINNER'S USER GUIDE

2024

ROBERT L. WALLEN

ROBERT L. WALLEN

QuickBooks Online 2024 Beginner's Guide

PennaDona
- PUBLISHERS -

Contents

Author's Note

Let's be real – accounting, no matter the software, has a reputation for being a snooze-fest. But hold on just a second, because with QuickBooks Online, that stereotype is about to get shattered. I know because I was once right there with you, drowning in receipts and spreadsheets, wishing there was a way to make sense of the numbers without wanting to tear my hair out.

It wasn't until I discovered the cloud-based wonder that is Quick-Books Online that I had my accounting "aha" moment. Picture this: I was managing a small café, and bookkeeping was a constant thorn in my side. Then I came across QuickBooks Online, and after some initial skepticism, I did try it out. Suddenly, those dreadful, time-consuming tasks started...well, to feel almost bearable. I could do them from my laptop in the cafe, at home on my couch in my pajamas, even on my phone while waiting in line. No more being chained to a single computer and a clumsy desktop software program!

See, QuickBooks Desktop, while a solid tool for many years, had its limits. It was like running a business on dial-up internet when there's super-fast broadband available. QuickBooks Online is that broadband – it's sleek, modern, and moves your accounting into the world of anytime, anywhere access. And here's the kicker – it's not just easier for folks who don't exactly love numbers, it's also powerful enough for experienced accountants.

That's why I decided to write this book. Not just to explain QuickBooks Online in a step-by-step way (though I do that too!), but also to share that sense of relief and possibility I felt when I first saw how much it could simplify my business life.

So, who's this guide for? Well, honestly, it's for anyone who does the books for a business and wants a solution that makes sense in today's fast-paced world. Maybe you're:

- **A small business owner:** You wear all the hats, and accounting is just one of them. You know it's vital, but you don't have the time or energy to wrestle with complicated software.
- **A freelancer or solopreneur:** Your passion is your work, not your invoices. You need something that's quick to learn and won't distract from your actual business.
- **A bookkeeper:** You might even be experienced with other software, but you're seeing the writing on the wall – the future of accounting is in the cloud.
- **A startup founder:** Your business is growing quickly, and the clunky old ways won't scale with you. You need streamlined, accurate accounting from day one.

Whoever you are, this guide is going to make QuickBooks Online your new best friend. We'll cover everything from the basics of what QuickBooks Online is and the exciting new features in the 2024 version, to setting up your accounts and understanding those all-important financial reports. We'll even dive into sales tax, payroll (if that's a need for you), and the more advanced stuff that helps power up your business insights.

And here's the thing: it won't just be dry instructions. We'll talk about the *why* behind every step – why things are done a certain way, and how all those reports and numbers actually tell the story of your business's health. We'll even tackle troubleshooting and where to get help if things don't go quite right. Plus, I'll sprinkle in some best practices I've picked up along the way.

Oh, and don't forget the bonus chapters! That's where we'll keep the super handy cheat sheets, and even give you some ideas about where to find more learning resources or free consulting sessions. Because, hey, we're all in this together.

So, ready to dive in and become a QuickBooks Online expert? Let's do this!

-Robert L. Wallen
[Author]

I

Introduction to QuickBooks Online

1

What is QuickBooks Online?

Hey there, ready to ditch the shoeboxes full of receipts and those dusty calculators? Let's talk about QuickBooks Online (QBO), your potential new best friend in the world of managing your business finances.

So, what exactly is QuickBooks Online?
Picture this: QuickBooks Online is like the super-smart financial brain for your business. It's accounting software, but way cooler because it lives in the cloud. Wait, what does that even mean? Well, instead of being installed on your computer like old-school software, it's all safe and sound on the internet. That means no worries about backups, no messy updates – QBO always has its thinking cap on.

Cloud-Based Accounting Software

Why does this "cloud" thing actually matter?
Here's the deal:

- **Work from anywhere, anytime:** Whether you're chilling on the couch, at a coffee shop, or halfway around the world (lucky you!), you can check in with your money situation as long as you have an internet connection.
- **Your accountant is suddenly your bestie:** Need your accountant's help? They can securely hop into your QuickBooks file remotely, making tax time a whole lot smoother.
- **Data, data, data, and it's safe:** All those bank transactions, invoices, and reports are automatically backed up and protected in the cloud. No more heart palpitations over spilled coffee near your computer.

Okay, but how does QuickBooks Online help my business?

You're busy running your awesome business, not stressing about numbers. QuickBooks Online swoops in to handle the nitty-gritty financial stuff so you can focus on the big picture. Here's what it's got:

- **Income and Expenses Made Easy:** Track what's coming in, what's going out. See where your money is flowing and make those money-smart decisions.
- **Invoicing Like a Pro:** Create sharp-looking invoices and get paid faster. QBO even lets you set up automatic payment reminders for those slightly forgetful clients (we all have them!).
- **Reporting Power:** Ever wondered which of your products is a rock star, or who your best customers are? QBO pulls all that data together in easy-to-understand reports. Become a financial whiz overnight!
- **Tax Time Zen:** QBO helps you stay organized, so when tax time rolls around, it's less about panic and more about simply handing things over to your accountant.

But hold on, isn't there a bunch of accounting jargon involved?

Nope! That's where QuickBooks Online shines. It's designed for folks like you – business owners who need powerful accounting without needing a finance degree. You won't see words like "debits" and "credits" thrown around – QBO uses plain ol' English.

Let's get real: Is QuickBooks Online *actually* easy to use?

Look, no one's going to say learning any new software is as blissful as eating a slice of cake (well, maybe some tech geeks). But QBO is surprisingly intuitive. It's filled with handy guides, pop-up explanations, and if you get really stuck, there's a whole community of QuickBooks users and experts ready to help.

Alright, I'm intrigued. Tell me more about this whole cloud-based accounting world.

Picture it like this: Traditional accounting software is like a typewriter – it does the job, but it's kinda clunky and outdated. Cloud-based accounting software like QBO is like your trusty smartphone - sleek, connected, and always evolving. Here's why the cloud is a big deal:

- **Automatic Updates:** QBO gets smarter behind the scenes. New features? They magically appear. Bug fixes? Handled without you lifting a finger.
- **Plays Nice with Others:** Got a favorite app for managing your projects or tracking time? Chances are, it talks to QBO. This whole "integration" thing means less jumping between programs and more streamlined workdays.
- **Ready for the Future:** As your business grows, QBO scales with you. Need more features? Upgrade your plan. The cloud makes everything feel a lot more flexible.

Think of QuickBooks Online as your sidekick, your financial mission control. It's got your back, so you can focus on doing what you do best!

Differences Between QuickBooks Online and QuickBooks Desktop

Alright, if you've been in the business world for a while, you've probably heard of QuickBooks Desktop. It's the classic accounting workhorse, installed right on your trusty computer. But with QuickBooks Online (QBO) shaking things up, it's time for a showdown: QBO vs. Desktop. Let's break down what sets them apart.

Round 1: Where They Live

- **QuickBooks Desktop:** This one's a homebody. You buy the software, install it on your computer (or a few computers in your office), and your data stays right there.
- **QuickBooks Online:** Lives in the cloud, just like your emails or online docs. You access it through a web browser. Your data? Safeguarded on super-secure servers managed by QuickBooks.

Round 2: Accessibility Smack-down

- **Desktop:** You're tied to the computer(s) where you installed it. Need to check something on the go? Tough luck unless you have fancy remote desktop software set up.
- **Online:** The world is your office! QBO works on your laptop, tablet, or heck, even your smartphone. Invoices on the beach? Why not! (Just watch out for those pesky sand grains in your keyboard).

Round 3: Updates and Backups

- **Desktop:** Updates are your responsibility. You usually buy new versions every year or so. Backups? Better remember to do them, or a spilled coffee could mean lost data.

- **Online:** QBO handles updates behind the scenes. New features and improvements? They just appear! And your data is automatically backed up.

Round 4: Collaboration

- **Desktop:** Designed for mostly solo work, maybe sharing files with your accountant at tax time. Real-time collaboration with others? Not really its thing.
- **Online:** Built for teamwork! You and your accountant can be in your QuickBooks file at the same time. Got a virtual assistant? Give them access too.

Round 5: The Cost Factor

- **Desktop:** It's a one-time purchase. But factor in the need for upgrades and the potential hassle of managing your own data security.
- **Online:** Subscription-based, you pay a monthly fee. This includes all those automatic updates, backups, and support.

The Verdict: So, which one conquers your financial world?

It depends on your needs! But let's move on to who QBO is really the perfect sidekick for...

Suitable Business Types for QuickBooks Online

QuickBooks Online isn't a one-size-fits-all solution, but it excels for certain types of businesses. Here's the scoop:

- **Businesses on the Move:** If you're rarely sitting at the same desk all day, QBO's flexibility is a lifesaver. Freelancers, consultants, anyone who travels frequently – you'll love the freedom.
- **Team Players:** Multiple people need to access your financials? QBO makes collaboration a breeze. Whether it's your business partner, your accountant, or employees, everyone can stay on the same page.
- **Tech-Forward Thinkers:** Desktop feels a bit old-school compared to QBO's constant evolution. Love the latest tools and features? QBO is always getting better.
- **Scalability Seekers:** If you dream of growing your business, QBO grows with you. Easily add more users or upgrade to plans with advanced features down the road.
- **Peace of Mind Enthusiasts:** The thought of losing financial data gives you nightmares? QBO's got your back with those automatic backups and top-notch security.

Not the Best Fit If...

- **You Crave Total Control:** QBO means trusting someone else (QuickBooks) to manage your data. If that's a no-go, Desktop keeps it all in your hands.
- **Customization is King:** Need super-specific industry features or heavy customization? Desktop offers more in this department.
- **Internet is Spotty:** Rely on a shaky internet connection? Desktop might be the safer bet, as QBO needs a good connection to shine.

Let's be real, choosing accounting software is no small decision. But hopefully, this breakdown gives you some serious clarity on whether QBO is your financial jam!

2

Benefits of Using QuickBooks Online

Accessibility and Convenience

L et's talk about why QuickBooks Online (QBO) basically gives you superpowers when it comes to managing your business finances on your terms. If you're tired of being chained to your office to check those numbers, this one's for you.

- **Your Office, Wherever You Are:** Say goodbye to lugging around a laptop with your financials on it. With QBO, all you need is an internet connection. Waiting at the dentist? Pull up your financials on your phone. Flight got delayed? Tackle some invoicing on your tablet. Your office is officially where you want it to be.
- **Data at Your Fingertips:** Need to look up an old invoice? Check on a payment? With traditional software, it might mean digging through files or firing up your office computer. QBO's search function is your new best friend – find what you need, fast.
- **Accountant Collaboration Made Easy:** Tax season used to be about frantic emails, dropping off shoeboxes of receipts, and general

panic. Now? Invite your accountant directly into your QBO file. They can see everything in real-time, ask questions, and generally make your life way easier.

- **App Benefits:** The QuickBooks app marketplace is like a candy store for your business. Time tracking tools, project management, specialized reporting...the possibilities are endless. Link these apps to QBO and suddenly you've got a custom-built system working for you.

Automation and Time-Saving

Think of QBO as your time-saving ninja sidekick. It's filled with clever features to tackle those boring, repetitive tasks so you can get back to actually running your business. Here's the magic:

- **Bank Feeds: The Reconciliation Revolution:** Manually entering every little transaction from your bank statements? So last century. Connect your bank accounts and QBO automatically pulls in transactions. Matching them to stuff you've already entered is a breeze, saving you hours every week.
- **Invoicing That Practically Runs Itself:** Set up recurring invoices for those regular clients, and QBO will create and send them automatically. You can even let clients pay directly online - cha-ching! Those late payments become a thing of the past.
- **Rules: The Robots Working For You:** Teach QBO your preferences, and it'll categorize transactions automatically. For example, tell it anything from Uber is "Travel Expenses." Less data entry for you, more time for that well-deserved coffee break.
- **Receipt Capture: Snap & Done:** Hold onto receipts? More like a fading memory. With the QBO mobile app, you snap a photo of a receipt and *boom* the expense is logged. No more digging through

your pockets at month end.

- **Mileage Tracking: No More Guesswork:** If you drive for business, the QBO app can automatically track your mileage. That means more accurate expense deductions and less headache come tax time.

But wait, there's more (seriously!)

These are just a few of the ways QBO streamlines your day. Imagine...

- **Inventory updates:** QBO can keep track of your stock levels, even nudging you to reorder when things are low.
- **Payroll on autopilot:** If you use QuickBooks Payroll, it integrates seamlessly with QBO–taxes calculated, paychecks sent, less stress for you.
- **Reports that run themselves:** Need a monthly profit and loss report? Schedule it, and QBO will have it waiting for you in your inbox.

The Real Payoff? Less Busywork, More Big Picture

Sure, learning any new software takes a bit of time upfront. But think of QBO as an investment. The accessibility and automation free up hours of your week. That time can go towards finding new clients, strategizing your next move, or heck, just taking a well-deserved break. With QBO, you're not just doing your books; you're taking back control of your time, and that's something no old-school software can offer.

Financial Insights and Reporting

QuickBooks Online (QBO) isn't just about plugging in numbers; it's about unlocking secrets that help your business thrive. Think of it as your financial crystal ball (without the cheesy music and questionable fashion choices).

- **Reports: Knowledge is Power:** QBO offers tons of built-in reports: profit and loss, balance sheet, cash flow... the classics are all there. But it's not just about the reports themselves; it's how easy they are to understand. Forget confusing accounting lingo – QBO reports use clear language and visuals.
- **Customization Galore:** Don't see the exact report you need? No problem! QBO lets you tweak existing reports or build your own from scratch. Want to track sales by product category? A report just for specific projects? It's all doable.
- **Dashboards: Your Financial Mission Control:** The QBO dashboard gives you a snapshot of your business health. See your key numbers at a glance – income, expenses, outstanding invoices, etc. Customize it with the metrics that matter most to you.
- **Trends Over Time:** QBO makes it easy to spot patterns. Are sales steadily increasing? Is there a seasonal dip in your cash flow? Understanding these trends helps you make smarter decisions for the future.

Why This Matters: Data-Driven Decisions

Let's be honest, staring at spreadsheets can make your eyes glaze over. QBO turns that raw data into something you can actually use:

- **Spotting Superstar Products:** Which of your products or services bring in the most dough? QBO makes it easy to see, so you can double down on what works.
- **Identifying Cash Flow Crunches:** Notice a pattern of expenses piling up at certain times of the year? You can plan ahead for that slow period.
- **Justifying Big Decisions:** Thinking of hiring new staff or investing

in equipment? QBO reports help you see if your financials can support that move.

Collaboration with Accountants

If dealing with your accountant used to feel like a game of telephone, QBO changes everything. It's designed to make teamwork with your financial pro a total breeze.

- **The "Accountant View":** Give your accountant secure access to your QBO file. They can work their magic directly in your data, no more sending files back and forth.
- **In-App Communication:** QBO has a built-in messaging feature for you and your accountant to chat right inside the software. Ask a quick question about a transaction, and they can see exactly what you're seeing.
- **Real-Time = Real Progress:** Your accountant can hop in and make adjustments, recategorize things, or prepare reports as they go. This means way less scrambling at tax time.
- **Advisory Power Up:** With up-to-date data at their fingertips, your accountant can go beyond basic tax filing and offer strategic advice throughout the year.

Security and Data Backups

Let's talk peace of mind. Trusting your sensitive financial data to a cloud-based software is understandable to be a little hesitant about. But here's why QBO lets you sleep soundly at night:

- **Security Pros on the Case:** QuickBooks has whole teams dedicated to data security. They use advanced encryption, constant monitoring, and all sorts of tech-wizardry that's way over our heads. But the bottom line: they take this stuff seriously.

- **Backups on Backups:** Remember those nightmares about accidentally deleting everything? With QBO, your data is automatically backed up constantly. One less thing for you to worry about.
- **Control is Key:** You decide who can access your QBO file and what level of permissions they have. Employees might only see certain sections, your accountant has broader access – it's your call.
- **Alerts & Monitoring:** If QBO notices unusual activity (like someone trying to log in from a weird location), you'll get an alert. It's an extra layer of protection against fraud.

The Takeaway: Protecting What's Yours

QBO understands your business financials are the lifeblood of your operation. Their security measures mean you can focus on running your business, not worrying about data breaches.

3

QuickBooks Online 2024: What's New?

4

Choosing the Right QuickBooks Online Plan

A bsolutely! Picking the right QuickBooks Online (QBO) plan can be tricky, so let's break it down to make that decision easier. Here's a look at how to choose the right plan and a handy comparison chart to guide you.

There's no one-size-fits-all answer when it comes to QBO plans. The best fit for you depends on several key factors:

- **Business Size and Complexity:** Are you a solopreneur with simple income and expenses, or a larger business with employees and inventory? The more complex your needs, the higher the QBO plan tier you'll likely need.
- **Feature Must-Haves:** Make a list of the absolute non-negotiables you need in your accounting software. Do you need to track inventory? Bill by the hour? Create detailed project profitability reports? This will narrow down your choices quickly.
- **Room to Grow:** Consider where you see your business in 1-2 years. If you're anticipating hiring employees or expanding your

17

services, it might be smart to choose a slightly higher plan than you technically need right now to avoid switching later.

- **Budget:** Of course, cost matters. QBO plans offer different features at increasing price points. Be realistic about what you can afford, but consider the time (and therefore money) you'll save by using the right tools.

Plan Comparison Chart (Simple Start, Essentials, Plus, Advanced)

Here's a breakdown of the main QBO plans with a focus on the key differences that will help you decide.

CHOOSING THE RIGHT QUICKBOOKS ONLINE PLAN

Feature	Simple Start	Essentials	Plus	Advanced
Price (approx)				
No. of Users	1	3	5	25
Income & Expense Tracking	✓	✓	✓	✓
Invoicing & Payments	✓	✓	✓	✓
Basic Reporting	✓	✓	✓	✓
Bank Reconciliation	✓	✓	✓	✓
Track Sales Tax	✓	✓	✓	✓
Bill Management		✓	✓	✓
Time Tracking		✓	✓	✓
Project Tracking & Profitability			✓	✓
Inventory Tracking			✓	✓
Batch Invoicing & Expenses				✓
Customizable User Roles				✓
Budgeting Tools				✓

Additional Considerations

- **Add-Ons:** Some features are available as paid add-ons for certain plans. For example, QuickBooks Payroll integrates with all plans but incurs an additional cost.

- **Promotions:** QBO often runs introductory offers or special discounts. Check their website before committing to a plan.
- **Accountant Access:** All QBO plans include access for your accountant – a huge time-saver!

Making the Final Call

Still unsure? Here's a strategy to help:

1. **Start with the "Must-Have" Feature List:** Eliminate any plans that don't tick those boxes.
2. **Consider the "Nice-to-Have" Features:** Would they make a big difference, even if not absolutely crucial right now? This can help justify upgrading a plan.
3. **Free Trial FTW:** Test drive the plans you're considering. QBO's free trials are the best way to see which one feels right for how you work.

A Note on Flexibility

The awesome thing about QBO is that you can upgrade or downgrade your plan at any time. So, even if you're uncertain about the perfect fit starting out, don't let that hold you back. Choose the best plan for your business today and know that you have the freedom to adjust as needed.

Let's delve into the nitty-gritty of selecting the right QuickBooks Online (QBO) plan based on your specific business needs. Understanding those limitations and aligning them with your business size is crucial for making a smart choice!

Deciding Factors Based on Business Size and Needs

Here's a breakdown of common business types and the factors that often weigh heavily on the best QBO plan:

Freelancers and Solopreneurs:

- Simplicity is usually key: You probably don't have complex inventory or multiple employees to manage.
- Focus on core features: Income/expense tracking, invoicing, tax prep basics.
- Affordability matters: Sticking to a budget while getting essentials is important.
- Potential Plan Fit: Simple Start is often a perfect starting point, consider Essentials if you need to track time for client billing.

Small Businesses (with a few employees):

- Collaboration features become important: Managing bill payments, tracking employee time, and maybe basic project tracking are helpful.
- Growing needs: Consider features that allow for expansion without switching plans later
- Automation for efficiency: Time-saving features are vital as your business grows.
- Potential Plan Fit: Essentials is often the sweet spot, Plus might be necessary if inventory tracking is crucial.

Established Businesses (multiple employees, potentially complex operations):

- Robust project management: Detailed tracking of income/expenses per project for profitability analysis.
- Inventory management: If you sell physical products, accurate inventory tracking is a must-have.
- Advanced reporting: In-depth insights for data-driven decision-making.
- Potential Plan Fit: Plus is a good starting point, Advanced usually makes sense for larger or more complex businesses.

Understanding Feature Limitations of Each Plan

It's important to remember, not every QBO plan is created equal! Here's where you need to pay close attention to avoid choosing a plan that leaves you feeling constrained later:

Simple Start - Potential Limitations:

- No bill tracking or management: Paying your own bills isn't directly trackable
- Limited reporting: Gives you the basics, but not in-depth insights.
- Single user only: If collaboration is needed, you'll need to upgrade.

Essentials - Potential Limitations

- No inventory tracking: Not suitable if you sell physical products.
- Less sophisticated project tracking: Lacks advanced profitability reporting found in higher tiers.
- User cap: Limits to 3 users might become restrictive as you grow.

Plus - Potential Limitations:

- Advanced budgeting tools: These are only found in the Advanced plan.
- Limited customization of user permissions: Less granular control compared to Advanced.

Advanced - Potential Limitations:

- Price: It's the most expensive QBO tier.
- Complexity: Might be overkill with too many features for smaller businesses.

Tips for Drilling Down on the Right Fit

- **Ask Yourself Honestly:** What tasks are currently causing bottlenecks or pain points in your accounting? Choose a plan that directly solves those problems.
- **The Future Vision:** Where do you want your business to be in a year? Two years? Factor potential growth into your plan choice.
- **"Nice-to-Have" vs. "Need-to-Have":** Be ruthless in separating these. 'Nice-to-haves' might tempt you to upgrade, but start with the essentials.
- **QBO's Help Resources:** They offer excellent comparison tools and articles on their website to clarify plan differences.

The Key Takeaway

Choosing the right QBO plan is an investment in efficiency and growth. Don't just think about where your business is *now*, think about where it's headed. Matching the right set of features to your business size means QBO becomes a powerful tool, not an expensive headache.

5

Navigating the QuickBooks Online Dashboard

T hink of your QBO Dashboard as mission control for your business finances. It's where you get a quick snapshot of how things are going, access important tasks, and find those crucial reports and tools.

Overview of the Homepage Layout

While QBO lets you customize your dashboard to a degree, here's a general overview of what you usually see when you log in:

- **Top Bar:** This is where you'll find the QBO logo, the search bar (your new best friend!), the "Create" (+) button for quickly making invoices, etc., and your account settings.
- **Left-Hand Sidebar:** The main navigation hub. Here's where you'll find sections like Banking, Sales, Expenses, Projects, Reports...all the key areas of your finances.
- **Central Area:** This is where the most important stuff lives:

- Snapshot Widgets: Boxes with key numbers (income, expenses, outstanding invoices, bank balances, etc.). Customize these to show what matters to you.
- **Task Reminders:** Bills to pay, invoices to send – QBO keeps you on track.
- **Insights Graphs:** Visuals showing things like your income/expense trends over time.

Key Navigation Areas (Banking, Sales, Expenses, etc.)

Let's do a quick breakdown of the most common navigation areas you'll find on the left-hand sidebar and what treasures lie within:

Banking

- Connecting Bank Accounts: The heart of QBO automation. Link those accounts!
- Transactions: See all those flows in and out, categorize them, and reconcile with your bank statements
- Bank Rules: Teach QBO to automatically sort transactions (saves *tons* of time).

Sales

- Customers: Your client database! Add details, track sales history.
- Invoices: Create, send, track, and get paid (the fun part!)
- Products & Services: Set up what you sell – this populates your invoices.

Expenses

- Vendors: Manage the people/companies you pay.
- Expenses: Log those business purchases, upload receipts.
- Bills: Track what you owe and schedule payments.

Projects (Plus and Advanced plans)

- Project Central: If you charge clients by project, this is your hub.
- Track Income/Expenses, profitability, and time spent per project.

Reports

- Report Library: Profit and loss, balance sheets, cash flow...all the accounting classics are in here.
- Management Reports (Plus and Advanced): Deeper dive reports for analyzing trends and insights.

Payroll (if you use QuickBooks Payroll)

- Employees: Manage your employee details, paydays, etc.
- Run Payroll: Calculate, pay, and file those taxes (and QBO does most of the heavy lifting).

Making the Dashboard Work for You

Here's how to ensure your dashboard becomes an indispensable tool:

- **Customize the Widgets:** Drag and drop the most relevant ones to the top. Hide the ones you never look at to reduce clutter.
- **Set Reminders:** QBO can nudge you about important upcoming tasks. Use this feature to stay on top of critical deadlines.
- **Explore Shortcuts:** The "Create" (+) button on the top bar lets you quickly jump into common actions like making an invoice from

anywhere in QBO.

- **Get in the App Habit:** The mobile app has a simplified dashboard view, perfect for checking those key numbers on the go.

A Note on Customization

While QBO allows some personalization of the dashboard, you won't have total control over the layout. The focus is on clarity and ease of use, ensuring you can find what you need without getting lost in a sea of options.

Customizing the Dashboard (Widgets, Shortcuts)

While QBO's dashboard is designed for clarity, you do have some power to personalize it. Here's how to make it work harder for you:

Widgets: Your Mini Info Centers

- Reorder & Resize: Drag and drop the widget boxes into your preferred arrangement. Some widgets can be resized to show more or less information.
- Add & Remove: Click the "Customize" button on your dashboard to see all available widgets. Add the ones important to you, remove those you don't use.
- Key Widget Recommendations:
- "Get Things Done": Reminds you of outstanding bills, invoices, etc.
- "Profit and Loss": A quick snapshot of your bottom line.
- "Cash Flow": Keeps an eye on money coming in and going out.

Shortcuts: Efficiency Boosters

- The "Create" (+) Button: This gem (top right corner) gives you quick access to:
- Creating invoices, estimates, and expenses.
- Adding new customers, vendors, or employees.
- And more, depending on your QBO plan.
- Keyboard Shortcuts: QBO supports several shortcuts. For example, CTRL+ALT+/ brings up the search bar. QBO has a handy list in their help section. There is a list at the end of this book.

Pro Tip: Tailor Your Dashboard by Role

- Business Owner Focus: Widgets like profit & loss, cash flow, and outstanding invoices live at the top of your dashboard.
- Freelancer/Project Focus: Consider a widget showing your time tracked for the week as a top priority.
- Bookkeeping Focus: Make sure widgets for unreconciled transactions and overdue transactions are front and center.

Using the Search Function

Think of QBO's search bar as your financial encyclopedia. It's shockingly powerful and can save you precious minutes (and headaches) trying to track down that elusive transaction or feature.

Here's how to master it:

Basic Searches

- Customer Name: Type in a customer's name to see invoices, payments, or contact info.
- Transaction Amount: Search for a specific amount to quickly find the related transaction.

- Report Names: No more hunting through menus for reports! Type "balance sheet" and it pops up.

Advanced Tricks

- Date Ranges: Search for "expenses January 2023" to narrow your focus.
- Filters: Start typing, and QBO suggests ways to refine. For example, search for "Invoice" and it'll offer filters like "overdue", "paid last month", etc.
- Natural Language: Often, you can type like you'd say it ("show me unpaid bills"). QBO is surprisingly good at understanding!

Why the Search Bar is Your Friend

- Finding Old Stuff: Need that invoice from six months ago? Search is way faster than scrolling through lists.
- Mystery Transactions: Notice a strange expense? Search by the amount for a quick clue.
- Learning QBO: Can't remember where a specific feature lives? Search often reveals it.

Power User Tip: Saved Searches

If you find yourself repeatedly searching for the same thing (like "unpaid invoices over $1000"), QBO can actually save your search criteria. Look for the little "Save Search" option once you've performed a search – it's a real timesaver!

Additional Considerations

- **Dashboard Changes Over Time:** As QBO adds features, new widgets and shortcuts might appear. Keep an eye on your options, especially after updates.

- **Role-based Customization:** If you have multiple users, each person can customize their own dashboard to match how they work within QBO.

II

Setting Up Your QuickBooks Online Account

6

Creating your Account

The setup itself is pretty simple. Here's the gist:

1. **Head to the QBO Website:** The place where it all begins! You can usually find the "Sign Up" or "Start Free Trial" button prominently displayed.
2. **Basic Info:** They'll ask for things like:

- Your Name & Email: For your login credentials.
- Business Name and Industry: Helps QBO tailor your experience a bit.
- Years in Business: Gives them a sense of your potential accounting complexity.

1. **Choose a Plan:** This is where things get interesting – we'll dive into that in the next section.
2. **Billing & Setup:** Pop in your payment info (if not a free trial), and QBO will walk you through a quick setup wizard to get the basics configured.

Choose Your Plan

This decision deserves serious thought, so here's a breakdown of what to consider, along with a glimpse into what you might find in each plan tier.

Key Factors to Guide Your Choice

Business Size & Complexity:

- Solopreneur/Freelancer: Often simpler accounting needs for income and expenses.
- Small Business with Employees: Payroll, more advanced billing features.
- Larger Businesses: Robust inventory tracking, project profitability analysis.

Must-Have Features:

- Income/Expense Tracking: This is core to all plans.
- Invoicing: A basic necessity for getting paid.
- Bill Management: Need to track what *you* owe?
- Time Tracking: Essential if you charge clients by the hour.
- Inventory: Only if you sell physical products.
- Project Tracking: For in-depth profitability analysis per project.

Room for Growth:

- Where do you see your business in 1-2 years? If scaling up, consider a slightly higher plan than you *technically* need right now. Saves the hassle of switching later.

Budget: Of course, price matters. Balance features needs with what you can afford.

Note: Prices and features can change slightly, so always check the QBO website for the most up-to-date info.

- **Simple Start**
- Best for: Freelancers, very simple businesses
- Expect Features Like: Income/expense tracking, basic invoicing, tax reporting essentials, connecting bank accounts, 1 user
- **Essentials**
- Best for: Small businesses needing some growth features.
- Adds Features Like: Bill management, time tracking, multiple users (up to 3)
- **Plus**
- Best for: Businesses that need inventory or project tracking.
- Adds Features Like: Inventory management, project profitability tracking, more users (up to 5)
- **Advanced**
- Best for: Larger or complex businesses.
- Adds Features Like: Advanced reporting and insights, customizable user permissions, batch transactions, dedicated support

Tips to Make the Right Call

- **Prioritize Needs:** Don't be swayed by shiny features you won't use. Focus on what solves your current pain points.
- **Take Advantage of Free Trials:** Experiment with a few plans to

see which *feels* right for how you work.

- **Don't Be Afraid to Upgrade:** If your business outgrows your QBO plan, you can seamlessly upgrade at any time.

Let's talk about those first few steps into your QuickBooks Online (QBO) world – signing up and following that oh-so-helpful Setup Wizard. Consider this your guided tour to get things started without a hitch!

Sign Up & Setup Wizard

The sign-up process and setup wizard are designed to be as painless as possible. Here's what you can usually expect:

- **Finding the Button:** QBO's website features a prominent "Start Free Trial" (or similar) button – that's your starting line.
- **The Basics:** Prepare to provide:
- Your name and email (these become your login info).
- Business name and what industry you're in.
- How long you've been in business (a rough estimate is fine!).
- **Plan Selection:** Choose your plan (Simple Start, Essentials, Plus, Advanced). Don't stress too much – you can change this later.
- **Payment Time:** If not during a free trial, you'll enter your payment info. QBO accepts most credit cards and sometimes offers other options like PayPal.

Enter the Setup Wizard

Once inside your shiny new QBO account, the friendly Setup Wizard usually pops up to help you configure a few initial things. Here's what it might cover:

- **Business Profile Deep-Dive:**
- Business type (sole proprietor, LLC, etc.): This impacts tax settings.
- Your fiscal year (when your accounting "year" starts and ends).
- Adding a logo: Personalize your invoices!
- **Inviting Your Accountant:** Get them in early to save headaches later. You'll just enter their email, and QBO handles the rest.
- **Connecting Bank Accounts:** We'll cover this more in a later chapter, but the wizard might prompt you to get started here to kick off the automation magic.
- **Quick Feature Walk through:** QBO might give you a brief tour, highlighting key things like where to create invoices or find reports.

Why the Wizard is Your Friend

- **Less Overwhelm:** Instead of a blank slate, it breaks down the first steps into manageable chunks.
- **Focus on the Essentials:** Guides you to the most important info QBO needs to work its magic.
- **Reduces Guesswork:** Makes sure your account is set up correctly from the get-go, setting you up for success later.

Tips for a Smooth Experience

- **Gather Info Beforehand:** Know your business type, fiscal year, and have your bank logins handy.
- **Free Trial First:** If unsure about the plans, try a free trial so you're not locked in immediately.
- **Don't Rush:** Take time to answer the wizard's questions accurately – this pays off big time down the line.

7

Connecting Bank Accounts and Credit Cards

T his process might seem a bit intimidating at first, but QBO has made it remarkably easy. Here's the general flow:

Link Your Accounts

Find Your Bank:

- From your QBO Dashboard, look for sections like "Banking" or "Connect Accounts."
- QBO partners with most major financial institutions. Use the search bar to find yours.
- Not seeing your bank? It might be supported, sometimes smaller banks are grouped under a generic "Other Financial Institution" option.

Secure Login:

- You'll be redirected to your bank's website or a secure pop-up window.
- Enter those same login credentials you use to access your online banking. Rest assured, QBO never stores your login info directly.

Choose Accounts:

- Decide which accounts to connect. Often, it's best to start with your main business checking, savings, and any credit cards used for business expenses.
- You can always link more accounts later if needed.

The Waiting Game:

- It takes a little time for the initial magic to happen. QBO needs to securely talk to your bank and download your transaction history.
- This can take anywhere from a few minutes to a few hours, so be patient!

Why This is a Big Deal

Connecting bank accounts and credit cards transforms QBO into a powerhouse because:

Automation Saves the Day:

- Your transactions flow automatically into QBO. No more manually typing in every little thing!
- This makes keeping your financials up-to-date a breeze.

Accuracy Boost:

- Human error alert! Manual entry is prone to typos. Automatic import significantly reduces those pesky mistakes.

Categorization Gets Easier:

- QBO starts to learn how you categorize things (e.g., that Starbucks expense always goes to "Meals & Entertainment").
- Over time, this means less manual work for you.

Reconciliation Magic:

- Matching your QBO transactions against your bank statements becomes infinitely simpler. This keeps your accounts accurate.

Important Security Notes

It's normal to be cautious about linking financial accounts. Here's why you can trust QBO:

- **Bank-Level Security:** QBO uses the same encryption and security protocols as your bank.
- **No Stored Credentials:** They never keep your login username and password on file.
- **Data Transmission Only:** QBO can only "see" your transactions, they can never move money or change anything in your accounts.

Troubleshooting and Things to Keep in Mind

- **Occasional Hiccups:** Sometimes the connection doesn't work on the first try. Check for any error messages and retry, or contact

QBO support if needed.

- **Initial Download Might Be Incomplete:** Often, banks only allow QBO to pull in a few months of history at first. Over time, more should become available.
- **Two-Factor Authentication:** If your bank uses this, you'll need to go through those extra security steps during the connection process.

Pro Tips for a Smooth Connection

- **Have Your Login Info Ready:** Avoid fumbling around for your bank passwords.
- **Start with One Account:** If it's your first time, linking one account first lets you get the hang of the process.
- **Check for Updates:** QBO sometimes needs to update its connection to specific banks. You'll usually be notified if there are actions you need to take.

The Magic Begins

Once your accounts are linked, the true benefits of QBO kick into high gear. Get ready to say goodbye to tedious data entry and hello to financial insights that flow into your hands with ease!

Alright, let's continue down the path of connecting your bank accounts and credit cards to QuickBooks Online (QBO). Now it's time to make some choices and understand what happens after you hit that "Connect" button!

Choose Accounts

After you've found your bank within QBO, you'll usually be presented with a list of your accounts. Here's how to decide which ones to link:

- **Business vs. Personal:** Keep things clean! Only connect accounts primarily used for business. Mixing personal finances makes things messy.
- **Checking and Savings:** Your primary business operating accounts are usually a no-brainer to connect.
- **Credit Cards:** Any credit cards where you regularly incur business expenses are great candidates.
- **PayPal and Other Payment Gateways:** If you receive significant customer payments through platforms like PayPal, connecting those is also helpful for tracking income.
- **The "I'm Not Sure" Scenario:** It's perfectly fine to start with a few key accounts and always connect more later. See how QBO handles the first batch, then make strategic decisions from there.

Initial Download

Once you've selected your accounts and completed the secure connection process, QBO gets to work behind the scenes. Here's what's happening:

- **Talking to Your Bank:** QBO establishes a secure channel of communication with your financial institution.
- **Grabbing the Data:** It requests a download of your transaction history. How far back it can pull varies a bit by bank, but it's usually at least a couple of months.
- **Patience is a Virtue:** This initial download can take a little time.

It could be a few minutes or a few hours – the best practice is to step away and let it do its thing.

What You Will (and Won't) See

- You'll see things like: deposits, withdrawals, purchases, fees – those core banking transactions.
- You usually won't see pending transactions immediately, those show up once they fully clear.
- Account balances might not be accurate right away, it takes a bit for everything to sync up perfectly.

Why It Might Not Be Instant

You'd think in this age of technology, things would be instantaneous. There are a few reasons for a slight delay:

- **Bank Cooperation:** Each bank has its own pace and security protocols for sharing data. QBO has to work within those systems.
- **Data Formatting:** Your raw bank data needs to be translated into a format that QBO can understand and categorize.
- **Protecting Your Data:** Extra time may be required to double-check that transaction information is accurate and secure.

Tips for a Smooth Initial Download

- **Avoid "Double Work":** If you've been manually entering some transactions, stop once you initiate the bank connection. Let QBO take over to avoid duplicates.
- **Expect a Little Mess:** The first download usually requires some cleanup. Transactions may need categorization or matching to things already in QBO.

- **Check for Errors:** While QBO is good, it's not perfect. Scan your transactions for anything amiss (incorrect amounts, missing items).

The Big Win

Despite a bit of waiting and potential cleanup, the initial download is where the magic of automation begins. Here's why it's worth celebrating:

- **The End of Tedium:** No more manually entering those daily expenses!
- **Data at Your Fingertips:** QBO turns those raw transactions into insights (how much did you *really* spend on office supplies last month?)
- **Tax Time Simplicity:** Accurate, categorized transactions make tax prep way less scary.

8

Importing Your Existing Financial Data

L et's talk about bringing your old financial data into QuickBooks Online (QBO). This is often a wise decision if you're switching from another accounting software or even from spreadsheets. However, it also comes with a few things to consider!

Here's a breakdown of when importing makes sense and when you're better off starting fresh:

Import If...

- **Switching Software:** You're ditching your old accounting program and want to preserve historical data in QBO for reporting and comparison purposes.
- **Tax Time Cleanup:** Your records are in spreadsheets, and importing into QBO will make tax prep way easier.
- **You Want Data Continuity:** Having past financial info in QBO gives you a better overall picture, even if it's just for reference.

Start Fresh If...

- **New Business:** No legacy data to worry about, so a clean slate is the simplest!
- **Major Process Overhaul:** You're using the QBO switch as a chance to revamp how you track your finances. Sometimes starting from scratch is better.
- **Messy Old Data:** If your existing records are full of errors and inconsistencies, it might be less painful starting with a clean QBO setup.

Import (If Needed)

Before jumping in, make sure you can even export data from your old software or your spreadsheets:

- **Software Exports:** Most accounting software has an "export" function. Look for options to export as a CSV file or one specifically tailored to QuickBooks.
- **Spreadsheets:** QBO can usually handle Excel files (.xlsx or .csv). The key is making sure your spreadsheet data is organized in a way QBO can understand.
- **"Oddball" Data Sources:** Not sure if your old format can be imported? QBO support has resources or might suggest workaround solutions.

Supported File Types

QBO is pretty flexible, but here are the most common file types it plays nicely with:

- **.CSV (Comma-Separated Values):** A basic text-based format ideal for spreadsheet data.

- **.XLSX or .XLS:** Microsoft Excel files.
- **QBO Files:** Files exported directly from another QuickBooks account.
- **Some Accounting Software:** QBO can sometimes directly import data from certain competitors' software (check their website for the latest specifics).

Preparing Your Data (The Not-So-Fun Part)

To avoid an importing nightmare, your data must be clean and organized:

- **Consistent Formatting:** Date formats, how numbers are entered...everything needs to follow a pattern.
- **Clear Headers:** In spreadsheets, the top row should label columns accurately (Date, Description, Amount, etc.).
- **Check for Errors:** Fix typos and weird things before importing – they'll only be multiplied in QBO.

Things to Expect During the Import Process

- **Guided Steps:** QBO has an import wizard that walks you through it.
- **Mapping:** You'll need to tell QBO which columns of your data correspond to its fields (ex: This column is "Payment Amount").
- **Not Everything Imports:** QBO can't handle super complex things like inventory with multiple warehouses or specialized accounting data.
- **Potential for Messiness:** Be ready for some cleanup work after the import is complete.

Tips for Success

- **Start Small:** If you have tons of data, try importing a smaller test batch first. Fix issues there before tackling the whole thing.
- **Get Help:** Your accountant might be able to prep your data or advise on a smooth import. QBO support also has resources.
- **Backup First:** Always save a copy of your original data before importing…just in case things go haywire.

Alright, let's assume you've decided importing your existing financial data into QuickBooks Online (QBO) is the way to go. Now we're going to cover the nitty-gritty import process and the crucial step of reviewing the results to avoid future headaches.

Import Process

While the specific steps might vary slightly depending on where your data is coming from, here's a general overview of how the import magic happens:

1. **Find the Import Function:** Within QBO, look for areas like "Settings" or "Your Company" and then sections named "Import Data."
2. **Choose Your Weapon:** QBO will ask what kind of data you're importing:

- Bank Statements (.CSV, .QBO)
- Customers/Vendors
- Chart of Accounts
- Invoices, bills…the list goes on!

1. **Locate Your File:** Select the file you've saved from your old

software or your carefully crafted spreadsheet.

2. **Mapping Time:** This is where it can get a bit tedious. You'll see your data and QBO fields. Your job is to tell QBO which is which. For example, your old spreadsheet's "Transaction Date" column maps to QBO's "Date" field.

3. **Deep Breath and Click "Import":** QBO will chug away, sometimes showing you a progress bar. There might be warnings or error messages to address if things aren't perfectly formatted.

Review Imported Data

Here's the thing: just because your data is *in* QBO, doesn't mean it's all correct. Taking time for a thorough review is crucial to avoid problems later.

The Sleuthing Begins - What to Check For:

- **Missing Stuff:** Did everything import? Sometimes certain transactions or old data get left behind. Spot check randomly across different date ranges.
- **Incorrect Amounts:** A classic import error. Scan transactions to ensure the numbers made the transition accurately.
- **Weird Dates:** Date formatting is a notorious troublemaker. Make sure transactions aren't weirdly showing up in the future or with the wrong year.
- **Duplicate Entries:** Check for duplicate customers, invoices, etc. These create a mess if not fixed quickly.
- **Categorization Chaos:** QBO tries to categorize based on keywords, but it's imperfect. Be prepared to manually correct many categories.

How to Hunt Down Import Errors

- **Sorting and Filtering:** QBO lets you sort transaction lists by date, amount, etc. This helps spot patterns (like a bunch of expenses with the same wrong date).
- **Reports to the Rescue:** Run basic reports like "Profit and Loss" for different periods. Do the numbers seem out of whack compared to your old records? This points to issues in the import.
- **Ask For Help:** If things are truly scrambled, enlist your accountant or reach out to QBO support. Sometimes a fresh pair of eyes is all it takes!

Cleaning Up the Mess

Depending on how successful the import was, you'll likely need to do some editing:

- **Individual Edits:** Click on any transaction to fix the amount, date, category, etc.
- **Bulk Edits (sometimes):** QBO has tools to change certain things across multiple transactions at once, saving you some clicks.
- **Delete and Re-enter:** For true import disasters, sometimes it's quicker to delete the incorrect transaction and manually add it the way you would normally in QBO.

Why Bother with This Potential Headache?

You might be wondering if the import effort is even worth it. Here's where it truly pays off:

- **Historical Comparisons:** Being able to casily compare this year's financials to last year's within QBO is powerful.
- **Tax Time Confidence:** If your past data is in QBO, pulling accurate

reports for your accountant becomes a breeze.

- **Cleaner Long-Term Data:** Fixing those import errors now ensures your QBO data remains trustworthy going forward.

9

Customizing Your Chart of Accounts

G et ready to delve into the backbone of your QuickBooks Online (QBO) system—the Chart of Accounts! This structured list of categories is where you track every penny that flows in and out of your business. Let's uncover how to customize it for a perfect reflection of your financial world.

QBO provides a starting point for your Chart of Accounts, but true power lies in tailoring it to match the nuances of how you do business. Here's how:

Understanding the Chart of Accounts

Think of your Chart of Accounts like a filing cabinet for your finances:

The Big Drawers: These are the main account types within QBO:

- Assets: What you own (bank accounts, equipment, etc.)
- Liabilities: What you owe (loans, credit card balances)

- Equity: Your stake in the business (owner investments, profits)
- Income: Money coming in!
- Expenses: Where the money goes (rent, supplies, etc.)

Folders Within Drawers: Each main account type is broken down into sub-accounts. For instance, your "Expenses" drawer might have folders like "Advertising," "Office Supplies," "Rent," and so on.

The Individual Papers: Within each folder are your individual transactions. An entry showing $100 spent on office supplies lives in the "Office Supplies" folder, within the "Expenses" drawer.

Why Customizing Matters

- **Organized = Informed:** A well-tailored Chart of Accounts translates your messy financials into clear insights. How much are you *really* spending on marketing? QBO can tell you with a click.
- **Tax Time Simplicity:** Your Chart of Accounts should align with tax forms. Having clear categories means less frantic scrambling when tax deadlines loom.
- **Unique = Better:** No two businesses are exactly alike. Your Chart of Accounts should reflect your specific income streams and expense types.

Tailoring to Your Business

Here's how to ensure your Chart of Accounts becomes a powerful tool:

- **Start with the QBO Default:** Explore the categories QBO provides as a baseline.

- **Add What's Missing:**
- Unique Income Sources: Do you offer a signature service? Create a specific income account for tracking it.
- Industry-Specific Expenses: Plumbers need a different "Supplies" category than freelance writers.
- **Get Granular (If Needed):**
- Break things down more: Instead of just "Advertising," you could have "Social Media Ads," "Print Ads," etc.
- Balance is key: Too many categories equals a cluttered mess. Find your sweet spot of detail.
- **Sub-Accounts Are Your Friend:** They add structure. A "Travel Expenses" category could have sub-accounts for "Airfare," "Hotels," "Meals," and so on.
- **Clean Up Regularly:** As your business evolves, so should your Chart of Accounts. Merge unused categories, add new ones…keep it an accurate reflection of your business.

Pro Tips

- **Account Numbers:** QBO assigns numbers to accounts. Strategically numbering things can create a structure for easier navigation and reporting.
- **Don't Fear Change:** You can edit your Chart of Accounts at any time. Experiment until it feels right.
- **Accountant Approved:** Your accountant is an invaluable ally! They'll ensure your Chart of Accounts supports accurate tax filings.

Examples of Customization

Let's make this real:

- **Freelancer:**

- Income: "Web Design Services," "Copywriting Services," etc.
- Expenses: "Software Subscriptions," "Hosting," "Continuing Education"
- **Retail Store:**
- Income: "Clothing Sales," "Accessory Sales"
- Expenses: "Rent," "Cost of Goods Sold," "Display Supplies"
- **Construction:**
- Income: Often broken down by job or project type.
- Expenses: "Materials," "Subcontractor Fees," "Equipment Rental"

Let's talk about two crucial aspects of customizing your QuickBooks Online (QBO) Chart of Accounts: ensuring it aligns with tax requirements and knowing when to call in your trusty accountant for guidance.

Tax Alignment

Nobody likes tax time surprises! A smartly structured Chart of Accounts can take a considerable chunk of pain out of the process. Here's how:

- **Know Your Forms:** Familiarize yourself with the tax forms relevant to your business (Schedule C for Sole Proprietors, Form 1120 for Corporations - your accountant can advise).
- **Matching Makes Life Easier:** Your QBO income and expense categories should broadly mirror the lines on your tax forms.
- **Example: Advertising Mayhem:** Instead of a single, vague "Advertising" expense account, consider:
- "Online Advertising"
- "Print Advertising"
- "Promotional Materials" This provides clarity you (or your accountant) will be grateful for.

- **When in Doubt, Ask:** Specific tax deductions can get tricky. It's better to create a QBO category with a question mark than to wing it and cause problems later.

Why Tax Alignment Matters

- **Less Stress, More Accuracy:** Mapping your Chart of Accounts to tax forms streamlines the process of gathering numbers for those filings.
- **Audit Protection:** If your accounts are organized in a tax-friendly way, it shows good faith effort should an audit occur (though they're still no fun!).
- **Confident Deductions:** Clear categories help you confidently claim all the deductions you're entitled to...because no one likes leaving money on the table.

Accountant Assistance

Accountants are your financial superheroes, and your Chart of Accounts is where they can channel their powers for your business. Here's when and how to enlist their help:

Best Times to Get Your Accountant Involved

- **Brand New Business:** Starting with their expert guidance ensures a rock-solid foundation in QBO.
- **Switching from Another System:** They'll translate your old data into a QBO-friendly format.
- **Big Growth Changes:** Expanded services or a new business structure might warrant revamping your Chart of Accounts.
- **Anytime You're Overwhelmed:** Feeling unsure is a great signal

to bring in a pro. Better to fix small things early than have a whole mess to untangle later.

How to Collaborate Effectively

- **Give Them Access:** QBO lets you invite your accountant as a user. The level of access depends on how involved they'll be in your day-to-day bookkeeping.
- **Be Proactive:** Don't just dump your shoebox of receipts at tax time! Regular check-ins ensure your accounts stay accurate.
- **Questions? Ask Them!** Your accountant can explain the "why" behind certain categories, deepening your own understanding of QBO.

Specific Accountant Awesomeness

Accountants can help with things like:

- **Complex Tax Rules:** Certain industries have niche deductions – they know what those are and how to track them.
- **Reporting Insights:** Accountants understand how to pull nuanced reports from QBO that reveal things average users might miss.
- **Projections and Planning:** Your Chart of Accounts data, in the hands of your accountant, can fuel forecasts for smarter business decisions.

The Power of Partnership

Some business owners worry that having an accountant means they don't need to understand QBO. That's a mistake! Here's why:

- **Control:** You're still the boss; the Chart of Accounts should reflect how *you* think about your business.

- **Daily Insights:** QBO is at its best with accurate, up-to-date data. That usually involves the business owner doing the day-to-day work, not just the accountant.

- **Better Conversations:** Basic QBO knowledge empowers you to ask your accountant intelligent questions and truly benefit from their expertise.

10

Setting Up Users and Permissions

Q BO understands that no two businesses (or even team
members) are alike. That's why it offers flexibility in
controlling who can see and do what within your account.

Manage Team Users

If you're not a solopreneur, here's the gist of adding your team to QBO:

1. **The Magic of Invites:** From within QBO's settings, you'll find
   sections like "Manage Users" or "Team." Here, you can enter the
   email address of the person you want to add.
2. **Choosing Their Role:** This is where you get to play gatekeeper!
   QBO has built-in roles or allows you to get super granular with
   custom permissions. We'll cover roles in more depth below.
3. **They Accept, You're Set:** Your team member will receive an
   email invite. Once they click and set up their password, they'll
   have access to your QBO according to the role you've assigned.

User Roles

Understanding roles is key to securing your data and encouraging smooth collaboration. QBO offers a few common ones, plus the ability to really customize:

Standard User: The basics for a team member:

- Can create invoices, enter expenses, run reports.
- Can't mess with most settings or delete important transactions.

Reports Only: Perfect for someone who needs an eye on the numbers, but shouldn't be fiddling with anything else.

Company Admin: The keys to the kingdom! This role has full access to EVERYTHING – proceed with caution when assigning it.

Custom Roles: This is where QBO gets cool. You can check boxes for fine-grained control. Accountant needs to see bank transactions but not edit invoices? Custom roles make it happen.

Why User Roles Matter

- **Security First:** Limiting access reduces the risk of accidental (or intentional) havoc being wreaked on your accounts.
- **Focus and Efficiency:** Someone doing data entry doesn't need to get lost in the advanced reporting weeds. Roles keep people on track.
- **Evolving Needs:** As your team grows, change roles easily. That intern who only entered bills now needs invoice access? Just a few clicks.

Tips for Success

- **Least Access Principle:** Start with the bare minimum permissions someone needs to do their job. You can always add more later.
- **Regular Reviews:** As your business changes, so might needed access levels. Audit your user settings every so often.
- **Accountant As Partner:** Your accountant is a special case. Discuss with them the optimal access level for effective collaboration.

Security Best Practices

While QBO prioritizes security, be proactive on your side:

- **Strong Passwords:** Enforce this for all users on your account. Avoid easily guessed passwords and change them regularly.
- **Offboarding Done Right:** Employee leaves? Immediately change their access to "inactive." No hard feelings, just smart security.
- **Be Aware:** Keep an eye on QBO's audit log to see what actions users are taking – a good deterrent against mischief.

Examples of Smart Role Use

Bookkeeper:

- Can handle day-to-day stuff: Invoices, bills, bank reconciliation.
- Shouldn't be deleting things or messing with payroll if an external service handles that.

Salesperson:

- Needs to create invoices, view customer info
- Probably doesn't need to see the full Chart of Accounts or run

complex reports.

Independent Contractor:

- Custom role is your friend! Perhaps they just need to enter their time worked and related expenses for easy invoicing.

Protecting your QuickBooks Online (QBO) data is just as important as the financial information it holds! Let's dive into security best practices and the unique considerations of giving your accountant the level of access they need to support you.

Security Best Practices

QBO has robust security measures in place, but as the business owner, you have an important role in keeping those virtual doors locked tight. Here are essential practices:

Passwords Are King:

- Strong and unique passwords for every QBO user. No "password123" here!
- Consider a password manager tool to generate and store complex passwords.
- Require regular password changes (every 3 months is good practice).

Two-Factor Authentication (2FA): An extra layer of security! QBO supports this. It requires a code (usually sent to your phone) in addition to your password when logging in. Highly recommended.

Mind Your Devices:

- Only access QBO from trusted computers and devices.
- Public Wi-Fi at the coffee shop? Bad idea for financial work.
- Keep antivirus software up to date on all devices used for QBO.

Beware of Phishing: Those emails from your "bank" asking for your QBO login? Fraud! Be vigilant, never click suspicious links, and always check the true sender of emails.

Stay Updated: QBO releases security patches. Enable automatic updates or check for them regularly.

Education is Key: If you have a team, make security a regular discussion topic. A single careless employee can put everything at risk.

Accountant Access

Your accountant is a trusted financial partner, and QBO makes it easy to securely bring them into your account. Let's break down the how and why:

Inviting Your Accountant:

- Within QBO, there's a dedicated section like "Manage Users" or "Your Accountant."
- You'll enter their email, and they'll get a link to set up their access.

Choosing the Right Level: Think carefully:

- Tax Prep Only: Maybe they just need end-of-year access to pull reports. Permissions can be limited.
- Ongoing Collaboration: More regular check-ins mean they'll need a broader range of access.
- Discuss it! Your accountant can advise on the optimal level for how you plan to work together.

Benefits of Accountant Access

- **Real-Time Support:** They can spot errors quickly, preventing headaches down the road.
- **Proactive Guidance:** Accountants often see patterns in your numbers that trigger valuable advice.
- **Tax Time Breeze:** With clean data available all year, tax filing is way less stressful.
- **Peace of Mind:** Knowing a pro has eyes on your accounts means you can focus on running your business.

Additional Security Considerations

- **Limit Admins:** The "Company Admin" role has all the power. Reserve this for only those who *truly* need it (including yourself!).
- **Communication is Key:** Open dialogue with your accountant about security expectations strengthens your partnership.
- **Audit Log:** QBO tracks user actions. Periodically reviewing this log can surface any unusual activity needing investigation.

Examples of Accountant Access in Action

- **Catch Those Tiny Troubles:** An invoice is accidentally coded to the wrong expense account. Your accountant can fix it before it warps your reports.

- **Planning Power:** Your accountant notices a trend in increasing costs and suggests proactive measures to manage it.
- **Tax Time Superhero:** Instead of scrambling to gather data, your accountant pulls accurate reports directly from your up-to-date QBO file.

The Responsibility Balance

Here's the thing: granting your accountant access doesn't mean you can completely check out of your finances. It's a partnership for a reason.

- **You're Still the Boss:** You should have a basic grasp of QBO and what's happening within your account.
- **Ask Questions:** Don't be afraid to ask your accountant to explain changes they've made or alert you to potential red flags.
- **Trust but Verify:** A quick scan of your transactions now and then ensures everything looks correct.

III

Daily Bookkeeping Essentials

11

Recording Sales and Creating Invoices

Creating Customer Records

Before those invoices can fly, you need to know who you're billing! QBO lets you maintain a robust customer database. Here's what you need:

The Basics:

- Customer Name (individual or business)
- Contact information (email, billing address at a minimum)

Go Deeper for Better Service:

- Payment terms (Do they always pay in 30 days? Note it!)
- Preferred payment methods
- Additional contacts at the company
- Any notes relevant to the relationship

Why Bother with a Database?

- Faster invoices: Instead of typing addresses every time, QBO will autofill.
- Track Sales History: See what a customer has bought in the past (great intel for up selling)
- Reporting Power: Run reports on sales by customer for focused insights.

Building Your Invoice

Now for the heart of the matter – creating invoices that clearly communicate what's owed and encourage timely payment. QBO makes this surprisingly customizable:

Start with a Template: QBO has several designs, pick one close to your ideal.

Your Branding:

- Add your logo for professionalism
- Color tweaks to match your brand are usually possible

Key Information:

- Invoice Number (QBO can automate this!)
- Invoice Date and Due Date
- Clear "Bill To" section with your customer's info

Line Items: The Meat of the Invoice

- Description of the product/service

- Quantity and Price
- Taxes (if applicable, QBO can even calculate this for you)
- Subtotals and the Grand Total due

Customization is Your Friend:

- Need a spot for purchase order numbers? Add a field!
- Early payment discount? Include a note on the invoice.
- "Thank you" message at the bottom builds goodwill.

Pro Tips for Invoice Success

- **Clarity is King:** Avoid jargon, make it easy for your customer to understand exactly what they owe.
- **Unique Invoice Numbers:** Essential for tracking and avoiding confusion.
- **Payment Terms Up Front:** Net 30, Net 15, Due Upon Receipt... state it clearly on the invoice.
- **Automate Where Possible:** QBO can send invoices on a schedule (great for recurring clients!)

Additional Features to Explore

- **Estimates:** Often a step before the invoice. QBO lets you easily convert estimates into invoices when the job is done.
- **Progress Invoicing:** Big projects? Break down billing into chunks within QBO.
- **Online Payments:** Integrate with services like PayPal to let customers pay directly from the invoice – speeds up cash flow!

Why It Matters: Invoices Aren't *Just* a Bill

- **Professionalism:** A well-designed invoice builds trust with clients.
- **Data Powerhouse:** Accurate invoices feed into those financial reports that guide your business decisions.
- **Cash Flow Hero:** Clear, timely invoices encourage faster payments, improving your cash position.

Now that you've crafted the perfect invoice with QuickBooks Online (QBO), it's time to get it out into the world and get paid! Let's talk about streamlined invoice sending and the all-important task of tracking payments.

Sending Invoices

QBO offers flexibility in how you deliver invoices, letting you tailor the approach to client preferences and your own workflow. Here are the main methods:

Email Straight From QBO:

- Most Common: Creates a professional-looking email, attaching the invoice as a PDF.
- Customization: Add a personalized message within the email.
- Instant Delivery: Invoice arrives in your client's inbox in seconds.

Get Fancy: Online Portals

- Upgrade Potential: Some QBO plans or add-ons offer customer portals. Clients can log in to view and pay invoices.
- Branding Boost: Makes you look super tech-savvy.

Snail Mail It (Yes, Really!)

- Print and Ship: QBO can format your invoice for a standard envelope.
- Old-School Clients: Some clients still strongly prefer paper.

The "Hybrid" Approach

- Email + Phone Follow-Up: Especially for high-value invoices, sometimes direct contact gives that extra nudge for payment.
- Emailed Invoice + Reminder System: QBO and some add-ons can automate emails like "Payment due soon!"

Tracking Payments

Knowing when money comes in is just as important as sending the invoice in the first place. QBO has your back:

Marking Invoices as "Paid"

- Manually Matching: When the money hits your bank, easily record it against the correct invoice in QBO.
- Bank Feed Magic: If you've connected bank accounts, QBO often suggests a match automatically.
- Partial Payments? No Problem: QBO can handle those too!

Reports to the Rescue

- "Accounts Receivable Aging": This report shows outstanding invoices and how late they are. Your collection hitlist!
- "Income by Customer": See who your best (and most delinquent)

paying clients are.

Why Payment Tracking is Crucial

- **Cash Flow Clarity:** Knowing *when* you get paid informs decisions about spending and investments.
- **Spotting Trouble Early:** A consistently late-paying client might warrant a change in terms (like upfront deposits).
- **Informed Collections:** Instead of nagging everyone, your reports show who truly needs follow-up.

Pro Tips

- **Payment Links Within Invoices:** Enable online payments like PayPal or Stripe for immediate payment options.
- **Late Fees (Use with Caution):** Can motivate some clients, but might damage relationships with others. Consider carefully!
- **Customer Experience Matters:** A gentle "Friendly Reminder" email is better than an aggressive "YOU ARE OVERDUE!" blast.

Additional Payment Features

- **Accepting Credit Cards**: QBO offers its own merchant services or integrates with others. Makes it easier for clients to pay.
- **Recurring Invoices**: For subscriptions or regular clients, automate the invoice creation and sending process.
- **Deposits:** If you require upfront payments, QBO can track these against specific invoices.

Invoicing Done Right Improves More Than Just Cash Flow

Here's a hidden benefit of a robust invoicing and payment tracking system:

- **Financial Health Check:** Is revenue steadily increasing? Are customers consistently late? QBO makes those patterns visible.
- **Pricing Power:** Your invoices hold data! Are your prices aligned with the value delivered? Reports can reveal this.
- **Client Insights:** Knowing who pays quickly (and who doesn't) impacts relationship building and even future sales decisions.

12

Tracking Expenses and Entering Bills

K nowing where your money goes is just as crucial as tracking income. Let's dive into how QBO helps you capture expenses and strategically manage bills.

Think of this as building the flip side of your financial picture. Every dollar out matters, so let's make sure QBO reflects them accurately!

Capturing Expenses

Life as a business owner involves spending. QBO's goal is to make recording those expenses fast and painless:

As They Happen = Best Practice:

- In the Field: The QBO mobile app is great for snapping receipt photos and entering the expense immediately.
- Back at Your Desk: Set a weekly time to input expenses, so things don't pile up.

Main Methods of Entry

- "Expense" Form: Detailed input with options for category, vendor, if it's billable to a client, etc.
- Bank Feed Magic: Connected bank accounts let you turn transactions directly into expenses.
- Receipt Snap: The app turns photos into expense entries (needs a bit of review to ensure accuracy).

Categorization is Key

- This IS Your Chart of Accounts in Action: QBO likely has defaults, but customize for what matters to *you*.
- Tax Prep Hero: Accurate categories map cleanly to your tax forms, saving headaches later.

Bills as Reminders

For expenses that aren't paid immediately, QBO's bill feature keeps you organized:

Why Use Bills (vs. Just an Expense)?

- Payment Due Date: QBO has reminders and reports centered around when bills need to be paid.
- Vendor Tracking: See what you owe to specific vendors, great if you negotiate payment terms.
- Approval Workflows: (In some QBO plans) – ideal if multiple people authorize payments.

Entering a Bill

- Similar to the expense form, but with a due date field and a place to attach the bill copy (PDF, photo, etc.).
- Mark as Paid: Once you've sent the check or online payment, mark the bill paid in QBO (essential for accurate reporting).

Pro Tips for Expense Success

- **Embrace the App:** On-the-go receipt capture and expense entry is an incredible time saver.
- **Little and Often:** 10 minutes a day beats a 3-hour monthly panic session with a stack of faded receipts.
- **"Unsure" Category:** Better to enter the expense with a "??" category than to completely forget it. Clean up later!
- **Link Expenses to Invoices (When It Makes Sense):** If you're billing a client for a specific expense, QBO lets you connect them for easy pass-through.

Why Bother Tracking All This?

It might feel tempting to just glance at your bank balance and call it a day. Here's why QBO's detailed tracking is worth it:

- **Real Profitability:** Knowing *exactly* what things cost reveals your true margins. Are you truly charging enough?
- **Tax Time Simplicity:** Organized expense records (with receipts!) minimize audit stress and maximize deductions.
- **Spotting Waste:** Those monthly subscriptions you never use? Reports highlight recurring expenses, prompting cuts.
- **Informed Spending:** Should you hire that contractor? Can you afford that new equipment? QBO reports turn gut feelings into data-backed decisions.

Bills: Your Cash Flow Control Panel

Bills in QBO become much more than just nagging reminders:

- **Upcoming Cash Needs:** Reports show what's due soon, so you don't get blindsided by big payments.
- **Negotiating Leverage:** Being able to pull a history of what you've paid a vendor strengthens your position.
- **Late Fee Debate:** Did they *really* charge you late fees consistently? QBO will expose that quickly to aid in the dispute.

Let's turn those stacks of receipts and jumbled expenses into a well-organized financial powerhouse within QuickBooks Online (QBO)! Proper expense organization streamlines processes, maximizes those tax deductions, and gives you the clarity to make better business decisions.

Organizing Expenses

Conquering your business expenses requires a two-pronged attack: a well-thought-out system within QBO and a way to get those pesky receipts into the digital realm.

Categorizing for Clarity and Tax Compliance

The heart of organization lies in your Chart of Accounts (those expense categories within QBO). Let's optimize it:

- **Start with QBO Defaults:** They provide a good baseline, aligned with common tax deductions.
- **Customization is Key:**Industry Matters: Plumbers need different categories than writers.

- **Level of Detail:** Do you need one "Supplies" category, or a breakdown of "Office Supplies," "Shop Supplies," etc.?
- **Your Accountant is Your Ally:** Ensure your categories make sense for tax filing and give you insights beyond just meeting IRS requirements.
- **Regular Reviews:** As your business evolves, so might your category needs. Adjust a few times a year.

Why Categorization is Crucial

- **Fast, Accurate Entry:** Clear categories minimize that "Hmmm, where does this expense go?" moment.
- **Powerful Reporting:** QBO lets you run reports by category... but those reports are only as good as the categorization itself.
- **Tax Time Hero:** When your accountant doesn't have to struggle deciphering your mess, you save on accounting fees too!
- **Uncover Hidden Spending:** Are those "Miscellaneous" expenses suddenly huge? Time to investigate what's hiding in there.

Receipt Capture

Receipts are the proof backing up your expense claims, and haphazard piles are a disaster waiting to happen. Here's how to tame them:

QBO Mobile App: Your Weapon of Choice

- Receipt Snap: Take a photo, it uploads straight to QBO.
- Matching Magic: QBO tries to connect receipts to existing bank transactions (gets better the more you use it).
- Notes Section: Add context to the receipt if needed ("lunch meeting with XYZ Company").

Email Forwarding:

- Some vendors email receipts. Create a special Gmail folder for them.
- QBO has a "Forward Receipts" email address. Batch-forward to get them uploaded in bulk.

The Old School "Shoebox" Method (Fine, But Not Ideal)

- Designate a Physical Inbox: At least they're contained!
- Regular Scan Session: Use a scanner or a good phone scanning app to digitize them and get them into QBO.

Retention Matters: Digital vs. Paper

- **IRS Guidelines:** Check their current rules on how long you need to keep backup for various expense types.
- **The "Just In Case" Factor:** Sometimes, even with a digital copy, you might need the physical receipt (product returns, faded ink issues).
- **A Hybrid System:**
- Digital-First: Aim to have everything scanned into QBO.
- Short-Term Physical Bin: For those few you might need the original of in the short term.
- Longer-Term Storage: Tax-critical items might warrant off-site secure storage (bank safe deposit box, fireproof home safe).

Additional Tips for Receipt Wrangling

- **"Pending" Folder:** Unsure what the expense is for? QBO lets you hold receipts until you've figured it out.

- **Travel Expenses:** These often have extra requirements. Create specific categories and consider an app specialized in this.
- **Automation Exploration:** Apps like Expensify integrate with QBO, adding features like mileage tracking and policy enforcement.

The Benefits of Organized Expenses

- **Audit Angel:** If the IRS comes knocking, clear expense records with backup make your life WAY easier.
- **Budgeting Power:** Not just guessing, but *knowing* how much you truly spend on things informs your budget.
- **Spotting Fraud:** Sadly, employee expense fraud happens. Organized records help catch discrepancies faster.
- **Data-Driven Decisions:** Is that monthly software subscription *worth* it? Expense trends inform those choices.

13

Reconciling Bank Accounts

Think of reconciliation as a financial detective game. Your clues are your bank statements and your QBO transactions. The goal is to make sure they tell the same story about your cash flow.

The Importance of Reconciliation

Reconciliation might feel tedious, but it's a non-negotiable task for accurate bookkeeping. Here's why it matters:

- **Error Catching:** Humans make typos! Maybe you entered $100 instead of $1000 in QBO. Reconciliation reveals these before they snowball.
- **Fraud Prevention:** Unfortunately, unauthorized transactions happen. Regularly checking your statements against QBO helps with early detection.
- **True Cash Position:** Your bank balance on a given day might not represent what's *really* available (checks pending, fees, etc.).

Reconciliation brings clarity.

- **Reporting Confidence:** Those QBO financial reports used for big decisions? They're only trustworthy if your underlying data is accurate.
- **IRS Happy = You Happy:** Auditors love clean, reconciled accounts. It signals good record keeping.

Connecting Bank Accounts

This is where the magic of automation begins. QBO securely links to most major banks and credit card companies, giving it a live feed of your transactions.

- **Find Your Bank:** Within QBO, look for "Banking" or "Connect Accounts." Search for your financial institution.
- **Secure Login:** You'll be asked for the same username/password that you use to access your bank online. QBO never stores these credentials.
- **Initial Download:** Depending on your bank, QBO might grab a few months of historical transactions – a head start!
- **Choosing Accounts:** Decide which accounts to connect (business checking, savings, credit cards are common choices).

The Matching Process

Once connected, QBO pulls in your transactions. Here's the reconciliation workflow in a nutshell:

1. **Side-by-Side View:** QBO shows your bank transactions on one side, QBO transactions on the other. Your job is to match them up.
2. **The Joy of Automation:** QBO gets smarter; often, it will suggest

matches automatically ("Hey, this $50 Starbucks on your statement looks like this $50 Starbucks you entered in QBO...are they the same?")

3. **Adding What's Missing:** Sometimes, you'll need to manually add transactions into QBO from your statement or vice versa.

4. **The Zero Dollar Difference:** When everything matches, your reconciliation is complete. A moment of financial zen!

Addressing Discrepancies

Real life is rarely perfect. Here's how to handle common mismatches:

- **Typos: The Bane of Our Existence:** Found a mistyped amount? Edit the transaction in QBO to make it match the reality of your statement.
- **Bank Fees and Interest:** Add these as transactions in QBO based on what your statement shows.
- **Outstanding Checks or Deposits:** Things in QBO that haven't cleared the bank yet are normal. They'll resolve in future reconciliations.
- **Uh Oh, Mystery Item:** Something on your statement you didn't record in QBO? Time to don your detective hat and investigate!

Pro Tips

- **Reconcile Regularly:** Monthly is ideal. The longer you wait, the harder it is to untangle messes.
- **Utilize QBO's Tools:** They have "help" articles and even short videos explaining the reconciliation process.
- **Unsure? Mark It:** QBO lets you flag discrepancies to revisit later, keeping you in the flow.
- **Accountant Assistance:** If things get truly scrambled, your

accountant can whip your reconciliations into shape.

The Reward: Financial Clarity

Reconciling bank accounts in QBO might not be the most glamorous task, but it's the bedrock of accurate bookkeeping. Here's why it's worth embracing:

- **Empowered Decisions:** Knowing your *true* cash position lets you invest, hire, or expand with confidence.
- **Peace of Mind:** No nagging doubts about whether your records are correct.
- **IRS Approved:** Clean reconciliations demonstrate responsible accounting, minimizing audit stress.
- **Catch Problems Early:** The sooner you spot errors or fraud, the easier they are to fix.

The Matching Process

The goal is to achieve that magical "zero difference": your QBO records align perfectly with your bank statement. Here's a breakdown of how matching works:

- **The Side-by-Side View:** QBO presents your bank transaction and QBO transactions in a clear format for comparison.
- **Automation Is Your Friend:** The more you use QBO, the smarter it gets about suggesting matches:
- **Similar Amounts:** A $25.45 gas station charge from your statement might be linked to your $25.45 "Fuel" expense in QBO.
- **Matching Descriptions:** If both the statement and QBO side say

"Acme Supplies," it's a probable match.

- **Manual Matching:** Sometimes, QBO needs your help. You'll have tools to select the correct QBO transaction to link to the statement item.
- **Adding What's Missing:**
- Bank Side: Fees or interest often need to be created as transactions within QBO.
- QBO Side: Did you record an upcoming rent check that hasn't cleared the bank yet? That's expected!

Addressing Discrepancies: Troubleshooting Mismatches

Even with careful bookkeeping, mismatches happen. Here's how to handle them like a pro:

- **Common Culprits**
- Typos: Did you enter $500 instead of $50 in QBO?
- Duplicates: Sometimes the same transaction gets imported twice, or you manually entered it and it came in from the bank feed.
- Timing Differences: Deposits made on the last day of the month might not clear until the next statement period.
- Uncleared Bank Items: Big pending transactions you've recorded in QBO but haven't hit your bank yet.
- Mystery Transactions: The "uh-oh!" moment where you see something on the statement and have NO idea what it is.

Your Detective Toolkit
QBO helps you track down the cause of discrepancies:

- **Sorting and Filtering:** Focus on a specific date range or transaction type (deposits vs. payments) to narrow things down.

- **Search Bar:** Look for a specific dollar amount or payee within your QBO transactions.
- **Flagging for Later:** Mark mismatches with a special status so you can come back without losing your place in the reconciliation workflow.
- **Notes Section:** Jot down observations as you investigate ("Maybe this check bounced?").
- **Don't Panic (Easier Said Than Done):** Even complex discrepancies can usually be unraveled with patience.

Troubleshooting Scenarios

Let's get practical with some common mismatch examples:

- **"$100 Charge on Statement, Nothing Similar in QBO"**
- Check Other Accounts: Could it accidentally be on a personal card you sometimes use for business?
- Bank Error?: Rare, but they do happen. Contact your bank to inquire.
- Fraud Alert: If truly unauthorized, take immediate action with your bank!
- **"Recorded a $2000 Client Deposit in QBO, Bank Shows $200"**
- Typo Likely: Double-check what you entered in QBO. Zeros are easy to miss!
- Partial Deposit?: Clients sometimes pay in installments. Could the rest be coming?
- Bank Hold?: For large or new accounts, banks sometimes have temporary holds.
- **"Multiple Small Fees on Statement, QBO Doesn't Match"**
- Lump Them: Create a single "Bank Fees" transaction in QBO for the total amount.

- Future Matching: As similar fees hit, QBO will get better at suggesting a match automatically.

When to Call in Backup

- **Truly Baffling Discrepancies:** If you've exhausted your sleuthing skills, don't waste hours. Your accountant can help.
- **Large Differences:** A few dollars off is often fixable. Hundreds or thousands might signal a bigger issue needing professional assistance.
- **Time Crunch:** If you're behind on reconciliations and tax deadlines loom, enlist help to get caught up.

14

Automating Recurring Transactions

B y setting up smart rules, QBO can handle a chunk of your bookkeeping for you, giving you back precious hours!

Automating Recurring Transactions

Think of this feature as your diligent robot assistant. QBO thrives on predictable, repetitive tasks like:

- **Recurring Invoices:** Clients billed the same amount with the same products/services each month (subscriptions, memberships, retainers).
- **Recurring Bills:** You pay the same vendor a set amount on a regular schedule (rent, utilities, some subscriptions).
- **Recurring Expenses:** Less common, but if you have expenses that truly are the same amount, scheduled recurring transactions can streamline things.
- **Recurring Journal Entries:** (Advanced QBO feature): Accountants use this for things like depreciation or spreading a prepaid

expense over time.

Benefits of Automation

Why let QBO take over these tasks? Because it translates to:

- **Time Savings:** Those hours spent creating the same invoice over and over? Reclaimed!
- **Accuracy Boost:** Less manual entry means fewer opportunities for typos.
- **Never Miss a Payment:** Automated bills reduce late fees and awkward vendor conversations.
- **Cash Flow Clarity:** Seeing upcoming invoices and bills scheduled in QBO improves financial forecasting.
- **Happy Clients:** Invoices arriving on time with professional consistency builds trust.

Setting Up Recurring Invoices

This is where most businesses find immediate payoff from automation. Here's the process within QBO:

1. **The Template:** Create a standard invoice, just like you normally would. Pay extra attention to accuracy – it will be used repeatedly!
2. **Turn On Recurring:** Look for the "Make Recurring" checkbox or option within the invoice creation screen
3. **The Schedule:** This is powerful:

- Interval: Monthly, weekly, even custom setups like "First Friday of the month" are often possible.
- Start Date: When the automation kicks in.
- End Options: Set an end date, let it run for a certain # of times, or

leave it open-ended.

1. Automation Options:

- Send Automatically: QBO emails the invoice to your client on the schedule…no action needed from you!
- Save as Draft: If you want to review it before hitting send, choose this.

Additional Recurring Invoice Tips

- **"Flexible" Recurring:** Need the same client invoiced, but the *amount* varies slightly? QBO can often handle that as a reminder to create the invoice, allowing final edits.
- **Customer Communication:** Let clients know you're automating their invoice for convenience.
- **Include a Stop Option:** In your invoice email text, remind clients how they can cancel the subscription through your website or by contacting you.

Setting Up Recurring Bills and Other Transactions
The process is very similar to invoices, with a few distinctions:

- **Recurring Bills:** QBO lets you automatically record the bill as paid if your bank account is connected and funds are guaranteed to be available.
- **Recurring Expenses:** Often tied to less-frequently changing things like yearly subscriptions where even the payment amount stays the same for long periods.
- **Recurring Journal Entries (Accountant Territory):** If you're not an accountant yourself, leave these alone! Incorrect use can

mess up your reporting big time.

Review and Adjust

Automation is amazing, but don't completely "set it and forget it".

- **Regular Review:** Quickly scan your "Recurring Transactions" list in QBO to make sure everything is accurate.
- **Pricing Changes:** Update recurring templates immediately to reflect price adjustments.
- **Client/Vendor Changes:** Cancel recurring invoices for ended subscriptions, update addresses or payment terms as needed.

Automating Bills

While getting paid feels fantastic, automating recurring bills tackles the other side of the cash flow cycle. QBO offers levels of automation to fit your comfort and workflow:

Level 1: Reminders Only

- QBO creates the bill for you on schedule (you fill in any changing amounts, etc.).
- Great for bills where the total fluctuates slightly from month to month.

Level 2: Auto-Enter and Pay

- Requires connected bank accounts and confidence that the funds are available.

- QBO records the bill and processes the payment... true hands-off!

Hybrid Option: Auto-Enter, Manual Pay

- Gives you control of when the money *actually* leaves your account while saving data-entry time.

Why Automate Bills?

Here's what you gain by letting QBO handle the predictable ones:

- **Avoid Late Fees:** Life gets busy, automating eliminates those costly "oops I forgot!" over payments.
- **Vendor Goodwill:** Reliable payments strengthen supplier relationships, which can be crucial when you need favors.
- **Reduce Stress:** One less thing to remember gives you mental space.
- **Budget Visibility:** Upcoming recurring bills in QBO factor into your cash flow projections.

Setting Up Automated Bill Payments

IMPORTANT: Proceed with caution! Only automate payments if you're 100% confident the money will be available in your bank account.

1. **Recurring Bill Template:** Enter the bill as usual, paying extra attention to the due date and any early payment discounts.
2. **Mark as Recurring:** Similar to invoices, you'll find the options to automate.
3. **Schedule and Settings:** Choose your schedule and whether QBO should just record the bill or process the payment too.
4. **Bank Account Connection:** For automated payment processing, link the correct account where the funds will come from.

Situations Where Bill Automation ROCKS

- **Fixed Predictable Bills:** Rent, phone service with a set plan, non-fluctuating subscriptions – perfect for automation.
- **Vendors with Online Pay:** QBO often integrates for seamless electronic payments.
- **Reliable Cash Flow:** If you're always confident the money will be there, automating saves time and hassle.

When Automation Might NOT Be Ideal

- **Fluctuating Amounts:** Utility bills (unless you're on a budget plan) are tough to automate fully.
- **Cash Flow Worries:** If things are tight, keep manual control of when payments go out.
- **Card-Based Vendors:** If your vendor prefers you keep a card on file with them, QBO automation might interfere.

Review and Adjust

Automation shouldn't mean you go on autopilot! Here's how to ensure your recurring bills stay on track:

- **Regular Review:** QBO has a section listing all your recurring transactions. Scan it often:
- Are the amounts still accurate? Vendors sometimes sneak in price increases.
- Any upcoming bills that will cause a cash flow crunch? Time to adjust!
- **Calendar Sync (Maybe):** Some users sync recurring bills with their personal calendars as an extra reminder.

- **Vendor Changes:** Update QBO immediately when payment terms or due dates change with a supplier.
- **"Just In Case" Buffer:** Even with automation, keep a small cash buffer in your account for unexpected expenses.

Additional Notes on Bill Automation

- **E-Bills and QBO:** If your vendor offers electronic bills sent directly into QBO, this further streamlines the process.
- **Not All Payments Are Equal:** ACH transfers through QBO are often slower than paying a vendor directly with a credit card (but check the fees involved).
- **Accountant Approved:** Before turning on automated payments, discuss your cash flow with your accountant to ensure it's a wise move.

15

Managing Inventory

I f your business buys and sells physical products, these features are crucial for tracking stock levels, understanding profitability, and ensuring you can always fulfill your customer orders.

Important Note: Inventory tracking capabilities are available in certain QBO plans (usually the Plus plan and above). If you don't see these features, you might need to upgrade.

Managing Inventory

Think of this chapter as building the foundation for knowing exactly what products you have on hand, what they cost you, and how much profit you generate from their sale.

Enabling Inventory Tracking

Your first step is to tell QBO that you want to utilize these advanced features. It's usually pretty straightforward:

1. **Settings and Gear Icon:** Within QBO, look for the settings area (often a little gear icon).

2. **Account and Settings (or Similar):** You're looking for sections like "Company" or "Account and Settings."

3. **Look for an "Advanced" Tab:** QBO sometimes groups these specialized features together.

4. **Inventory Toggle:** There will be a clear checkbox or toggle switch to turn inventory tracking ON.

5. **Save and You're Ready:** Make sure to hit that save button after making the change.

Adding Inventory Items

With inventory activated, it's time to populate QBO with your products. Here's how to do it thoughtfully:

- **The Product Record:** Think of this as your inventory item's file:
- SKU (Stock Keeping Unit): A unique identifier you assign. Make it logical for how you think about your products.
- Product Name: What you and your customers call it.
- Description: Enough detail for accurate sales and ordering, but not overwhelming.
- Category: Start building your inventory hierarchy (ex: Clothing > Shirts > Short Sleeve)
- Initial Quantity: How many do you have on hand right now?
- Reorder Point: (We'll cover this later!) A trigger for when to buy more.
- **The "Cost" Component** (Crucial!)
- Purchase Price: What you pay your supplier per unit.
- Income Account: This links inventory to your Chart of Accounts for accurate reporting.
- Expense Account: Where QBO records the cost when the item is sold (usually "Cost of Goods Sold").

Why Bother with Detailed Inventory Records?
It might feel tempting to just put in basic product names and call it a day. Here's why taking the time to set it up right pays off:

- **Accurate COGS:** Cost of Goods Sold is a key part of your profitability picture. Sloppy inventory = sloppy financials, which leads to bad decisions.
- **Stock Levels at a Glance:** Know instantly how many you can sell without a frantic search through the warehouse.
- **Reorder Smarts:** QBO can alert you when it's time to restock, preventing disappointing customers with "out of stock" notices.
- **Reporting Power:** Instead of just seeing overall sales, drill down into profitability by product or product category.

Additional Inventory Setup Considerations

- **Photos:** Make it visual! Especially if you have similar items, a photo reduces picking errors when fulfilling orders.
- **Multiple Vendors/Pricing:** Some QBO plans let you track multiple suppliers for a single product and compare pricing.
- **Bar code Integration:** If you have a bar code system, QBO sometimes integrates for easy updates when scanning items in or out.
- **Assembly Builds (Advanced):** If you create finished products from component parts, QBO offers "assembly" builds to track those materials properly.

Pro Tips

- **Physical Count Accuracy:** Even with QBO, doing a regular physical inventory count is vital to catch discrepancies (theft, damage, etc.).

- **Don't Over complicate:** Start with your most important products, perfect the setup, then gradually add more.
- **Label Everything Clearly:** Your warehouse organization system should mirror your QBO product names/SKUs to streamline picking.

Now that you've mastered setting up your inventory in QuickBooks Online (QBO), let's explore how those day-to-day sales and purchasing activities interact with your inventory records. We'll also unveil the power of inventory reports!

Sales Impact on Inventory

The heart of inventory management is understanding how sales affect your stock levels. QBO does the heavy lifting behind the scenes:

- **The Magic of Invoices:** When you create an invoice that includes inventory items:
- QBO automatically reduces the quantity on hand of that item.
- The value of the item (based on your cost) flows through to your Cost of Goods Sold.
- You have an accurate, real-time picture of what's left.
- **Why It Matters**
- Prevents Overselling: QBO can alert you if you try to invoice more of a product than you have.
- Data-Driven Restock: Knowing what's selling quickly guides your purchasing decisions.
- Accurate Profitability: Without the sales-inventory link, your profit margins are just a guess.

Purchase Orders

The flip-side of selling is restocking. QBO's purchase order (PO) feature helps manage this process:

Creating a PO: Think of it as the order you send to your supplier.

- Select Vendor: QBO can pull in their contact information.
- Items: Choose your inventory items, quantities, and confirm the pricing.
- Expected Delivery: Setting an approximate date provides tracking.

POs Aren't Just Paperwork:

- Track What's Due: See what you have on order but haven't received yet.
- Receive Against POs: When the shipment arrives, QBO lets you easily mark items received, automatically increasing your inventory quantity on hand.
- Partial Shipments: No problem! You can receive a portion of the PO now and the rest later.

Why Use POs within QBO?

- **Vendor Accountability:** Having the PO in your system lets you easily follow up on late or incorrect orders.
- **Inventory Forecasting:** Seeing upcoming POs helps you anticipate stock needs, especially for big sales pushes.
- **Bill Matching:** When the bill from the vendor arrives, QBO simplifies matching it to the PO, ensuring the pricing is as agreed.
- **Approval Workflows (Advanced):** Some QBO plans let you set

up rules where POs require management approval before being sent.

Inventory Reports

QBO takes the data from your sales and purchase activities and turns it into actionable insights. Here's a taste of the inventory reports to explore:

Inventory Valuation Summary:

- The Current $ Value: Shows the total dollar value of the inventory you have on hand. Vital for things like insurance purposes.
- Quantity on Hand: A quick snapshot of stock levels by item.

Inventory Stock on Hand:

- Drill-Down: Click on specific items to see the detailed transaction history (sales decreasing it, POs increasing it).

Product Profitability:

- The Star Performers: Which items generate the most profit, not just the greatest revenue? This helps focus your efforts.

Reorder Point Alerts:

- * Never Run Out: QBO can warn you when items fall below your preset reorder threshold.

Pro Tips

- **Cycle Counts:** Instead of a full inventory shutdown, do mini-counts of certain products regularly – improves accuracy over time.
- **Inventory Adjustments:** Damage, shrinkage, etc., happen. QBO lets you record those adjustments to keep quantities accurate.
- **"Assembly" Items (Advanced):** If you build finished goods from raw materials, QBO has features to manage that process with automated impact on ingredient inventory.

The Takeaway

By diligently using QBO's invoices, purchase orders, and leveraging its insightful inventory reports, you gain unprecedented control over your physical products. This control translates into:

- **Delighting Customers:** Always having the items they want in stock.
- **Less Waste:** Avoid overbuying and the dreaded pile of slow-moving inventory.
- **Maximized Profits:** Spot your most profitable items and ensure you can keep up with demand.
- **Peace of Mind:** Knowing your inventory records are accurate reduces a major source of business owner stress.

Let QBO be your tireless inventory assistant, keeping track of every item that comes in and goes out, so you can focus on the big-picture growth of your business.

IV

Mastering Customer and Vendor Management

16

Adding and Managing Customer Information

A dding a new customer in QBO is like setting up their dedicated file within your system. Here's how to find and fill in the various sections:

- **"Customers" or "Sales" Hub:** QBO usually has a primary area where your customer list lives. Look for these or similar terms in the navigation.
- **The "Add Customer" Button:** Pretty self-explanatory! Clicking this initiates the process.
- **Company vs. Individual:** QBO can handle both. Choose the one that matches your customer.
- **Display Name:** How you want this customer to appear on invoices, reports, etc.

Creating Comprehensive Customer Records

QBO provides a solid baseline of fields, but the true power comes in making it work for *your* business's unique needs. Here's the core data to include:

- **Basic Contact Info:**
- Name (and contact person if a company)
- Billing Address (and shipping address if different)
- Email (ideally multiple contacts at a company if you have them)
- Phone Numbers
- **Payment & Billing:**
- Payment Terms (Net 30, etc.): Ensures invoices are generated with the correct due dates.
- Preferred Payment Method: Helps tailor your collections approach.
- Tax ID If Applicable: If the customer is exempt, storing their Tax ID makes sales tax reporting easier.
- **Notes:**
- A catch-all! Special instructions, reminders of their preferred product types, any details that aid in better service go here.

Customizing Customer Fields for Tailored Data

This is where QBO starts to feel like it was built *just for you*. Here's how to add your own specific fields:

1. **Gear Icon (Settings):** Look for areas like "Company Settings."
2. **Sales Forms or Similar:** QBO often groups customization of forms (invoices, etc.) together, including the underlying customer data fields.
3. **Custom Fields:** You'll be able to add new fields of various types:

- Text: Short bits of data
- Number: Great for things like customer loyalty numbers or internal ID systems
- Dropdowns: Create lists of choices for quick entry (example: Customer Type - Retail, Wholesale, etc.)

Why Invest Time in Detailed Customer Records?

Targeted Sales & Marketing:

- Customer Type: Different messages might resonate with different customer segments.
- Last Purchase Date: Spot "lapsed" customers for win-back campaigns.
- Interest Fields: Track what products they like so your emails feel relevant, not spammy.

Personalized Customer Service:

- Quick Answers: See a customer's preferred shipping method right in their record – cuts down on back-and-forth.
- Build Relationships: The Notes field can even store their dog's name for a personal touch in conversations.

Smart Financial Decisions:

- Creditworthiness: Combine payment terms and payment history notes to assess risk when extending larger lines of credit.
- Sales Patterns: Do certain customers only buy when there's a discount? Informs your pricing strategy.

Pro Tips

- **Consistency is Key:** Train your team on how to fill out fields and the importance of accurate data entry.
- **Set Required Fields:** QBO can enforce that certain fields must be filled out, improving data quality.
- **Review & Clean Up:** Schedule time (quarterly is good) to check for incomplete records or merge accidental duplicates.

Managing Customer Contacts and Multiple Addresses

Especially within B2B sales, you're rarely dealing with just a single person at your customer's company. Here's how QBO helps keep track of the whole crew:

Sub-Customers (Sometimes): Some QBO plans allow adding "child" records under the main customer.

- Pros: Keeps info together, ideal if different people need their own invoices within a single larger account.
- Cons: Can slightly clutter your main customer list.

Contacts Tab WITHIN the Customer Record

- The Better Approach: Most users find this the most streamlined solution.
- Each Contact: Gets their own name, email, phone, etc. fields.
- Invoicing Power: When creating an invoice, QBO lets you choose

which contact the invoice should be addressed to.

Shipping vs. Billing Address

- QBO accommodates this! Separate fields for each purpose.
- Streamlined Fulfillment: If you ship products, this ensures no confusion on where they need to go.
- Reporting: Some QBO reports can even break down sales by ship-to location.

Scenario: Selling to a Large Company
You might have contacts like this within a single customer record in QBO:

- **Main Contact:** Kathy in Accounting – gets the invoices
- **Purchasing Agent:** Steve, who actually places the orders
- **Warehouse Manager:** Joe, who needs shipping notifications

Categorizing Customers for Targeted Communication

Let's turn those customer records into marketing gold. QBO might not be a full-fledged CRM, but it offers basic tools to segment your audience:

Built-In Tools:

- Customer Type Field: Use the customization feature to make this a drop down with your own categories (Retail, Non-Profit, Government, etc.).
- Tagging: Some QBO versions have a simple tagging feature, letting

you add free form tags ("High Value Client," "Lapsed Customer," etc.).

Getting Creative with Notes

- If your QBO plan is limited, a well-structured Notes field can work. Example: NOTE: Industry - Manufacturing | Interest - Widget 2000
- Requires Discipline: Train your team on the exact format, otherwise, it becomes a jumbled mess

Export and Enhance

- QBO lets you export customer data. Using a spreadsheet or dedicated email tool then provides more powerful filtering/grouping.

Why Categorization Matters

- **Focused Messaging:** Don't blast everyone with the same generic promotion.
- **Industry-Specific Offers:** Deals relevant to their field get way better engagement.
- **Purchase Behavior:** Promote complementary products based on what they've previously bought.
- **Customer Experience Boost:** Emails that feel personalized increase goodwill and loyalty.
- **Save Time and Money:** Targeted campaigns mean you're not wasting efforts on customers unlikely to be interested.

Examples of Customer Categorization in Action

- **Wholesaler vs. End-User:** Pricing, product descriptions in invoices, and even follow-up cadence might be different for these groups.
- **Large vs. Small Spenders:** Focus your top-notch customer service efforts on those high-value clients.
- **Geography Matters:** Useful if you have location-specific promotions or need to factor shipping costs into your sales approach.

Pro Tips

- **Start Simple:** Better to have a few well-used categories than an overwhelming system no one uses consistently.
- **Involve Your Sales Team:** They have on-the-ground insights about how customers differ that can inform your category choices.
- **Tie It Back to Goals:** Are you trying to grow a certain market segment? Create a category to support those specific outreach efforts.

17

Adding and Managing Vendor Information

L et's shift our focus from the customer side to mastering vendor management within QuickBooks Online (QBO). Robust vendor records are just as crucial to your business success, ensuring you have the supplies and services you need, at the right price, and with smooth payment processes.

Similar to customers, QBO provides a central hub to manage your suppliers. Look for areas marked:

- **Vendors**
- **Expenses**
- **Suppliers**

Within this hub, you'll find the options to "Add Vendor" and start building their profile.

Establishing Detailed Vendor Profiles

The core details QBO will need for each vendor include:

Basics

- Company Name (or individual's name if a freelancer)
- Primary Contact: Who you call to place orders or with questions
- Full Address: Required for generating bills and sending payments
- Email & Phone: Multiple contact methods are always wise

Financial Must-Haves:

- Payment Terms: How long you have to pay them (Net 15, Net 30, etc.) Crucial for cash flow planning.
- Tax Information:
- Do you need to issue them a 1099 at year-end? QBO can be set up to track this.
- If they charge sales tax, make sure that's captured correctly on your bills.
- Default Expense Account: When you enter a bill from this vendor, QBO will auto-suggest an account to speed up the process.

The "Nice to Haves"

- Website: Great for quick reference when reordering, etc.
- Account Numbers: Any internal ID systems your vendor uses – speeds up communication if there's an issue.
- Notes: Special terms, warnings ("Always ship overnight!"), or even a preferred rep's name can go here.

Tracking Vendor Contact Information and Payment Terms

Let's zero in on two critical elements within the vendor record that directly impact your payable process and, ultimately, your business's reputation.

Contacts (Similar to Customers)

- Beyond the Main: Perhaps you have an alternate contact person for emergencies or a specific email address for invoices only.
- QBO Power: When creating a bill, you can easily select which contact it should be addressed to.

Payment Terms: The Impact

- Invoice Due Dates: QBO factors in those payment terms automatically when you create a bill.
- Cash Flow Clarity: Upcoming bills reports in QBO show the due date, giving you a true cash flow picture.
- Collections Connection: Overdue payments become obvious, letting you prioritize those vendor conversations.
- Vendor Goodwill: Consistently meeting payment terms builds a positive relationship.

Why Detailed Vendor Records Matter

It's tempting to just slap in a vendor's name and call it good. Here's why taking the extra time pays off:

- **No Last-Minute Scrambles:** Ever had the "where's that invoice?!" panic in Accounts Payable? A detailed vendor record in QBO prevents that.

- **Negotiation Leverage:** Being able to quickly pull a history of your purchases from a vendor gives you power when discussing pricing or contract terms.
- **Spot Cost Increases:** Is a key supplier subtly raising prices? QBO reports broken down by vendor reveal those trends.
- **Reduce Errors:** Accurate payment addresses and contact info mean fewer delays or misdirected payments that damage the relationship.
- **Audit Protection:** In the unfortunate event of an IRS audit, clear vendor records demonstrate responsible financial management.

Pro Tips

- **Attachment Power:** QBO lets you upload files to vendor records. Scanned contracts, W-9s, etc. keep everything centralized.
- **Vendor Performance Notes:** Track things like on-time delivery rates or quality issues. Informs future supplier decisions.
- **Inactivate Old Vendors:** Declutter your list by marking no-longer-used suppliers as inactive. You can always reactivate them later if needed.

Categorizing Vendors for Streamlined Spending Analysis

Just like with customers, segmenting your vendors unlocks valuable insights about where your money is going. Here's how:

Vendor Type Field:

- Customize It: Set up a drop down with categories like "Raw Materials," "Office Supplies," "Marketing Services," etc.
- Match Your Chart of Accounts: Aligning vendor categories with your expense accounts supercharges reporting.

Tagging (If Supported):

- Adds Flexibility: Some QBO plans offer tagging for vendors.
- Examples: "Preferred Vendor," "Minority-Owned," "Local Business" – whatever matters to your tracking efforts.

The Power of QBO Reporting

- Spend by Category: See at a glance where the largest chunk of your expenses goes – informs sourcing decisions.
- Vendor Detail: Drill down to see exactly which vendors within a category are driving the majority of the costs.
- Spotting Waste: That "Miscellaneous" category suddenly huge? Dig in to uncover potentially unnecessary spending.

Real-World Examples of Vendor Categorization

- **Manufacturing Business:**
- "Direct Materials" vs. "Indirect Materials" helps calculate true product costs for accurate pricing.
- Tagging a vendor as "Single Source" highlights supply chain risk and prompts a search for backups.
- **Service-Based Business**
- Categorize by project type: Helps assess true profitability of different service offerings.
- Tagging "Freelancer" vs. "Agency" aids in budgeting decisions.

Storing Vendor Contracts and Legal Documents

QBO, while not a full-fledged document management system, offers a few ways to keep contracts and other important vendor documents centralized:

Attachments on the Vendor Record

- Scanned PDFs: Simple and effective. Name files clearly ("Vendor X Contract 2023.pdf") to avoid confusion.
- QBO limits individual file sizes, so break up large contracts into multiple uploads if needed.

Notes Field Workaround

- Copy/Paste: If the document is purely text-based, pasting it directly into the Notes field works, but gets messy for complex documents.
- Links: Store the contract in a cloud drive (Dropbox, etc.) and add the link to the Notes field for quick access.

External Integration

- Apps Galore: QBO integrates with various cloud storage and document management tools, offering more robust features like version control.
- Security Considerations: Research the app's security measures, especially if dealing with sensitive contracts.

Why Centralizing Vendor Docs in QBO Matters

- **Renewal Time = No Panic:** Expiring contracts are easy to spot if stored alongside the vendor info in QBO.
- **Disputes Made Simpler:** Having the contract readily accessible in QBO prevents those "they said, we said" arguments.
- **Informed Vendor Choices:** Referencing past contracts when renegotiating or seeking new suppliers gives you the upper hand.
- **Audit Shield:** Organized contract records demonstrate due diligence to an auditor.

Additional Considerations

- **Access Control:** Some QBO plans let you manage user permissions. Consider limiting sensitive contract access to only those who truly need it.
- **Version Control:** If contracts are under frequent revision, an external tool with versioning features might be necessary to avoid confusion.
- **Backup, Backup, Backup:** While QBO is secure, having your own independent backup of critical contracts is always wise.

18

Creating Estimates and Purchase Orders

L et's dive into the world of estimates and purchase orders within QuickBooks Online (QBO) – the tools that streamline your sales and procurement processes respectively. We'll cover how to create professional-looking documents and leverage their time-saving potential.

- **Estimates**
- Often Found Under: "Sales" or "Customers" tabs. QBO groups sales-related workflows together.
- Button Action: Look for "Create Estimate" or something similar.
- **Purchase Orders**
- Usually Located: Under "Expenses," "Vendors," or even its own dedicated "POs" area.
- Creation: Similar to estimates, there will be a clear option to start a new PO.

Generating Professional Estimates for Customer Approval

Estimates are key to setting expectations and winning the job. Here's how QBO elevates them beyond mere scraps of paper:

Customization is Your Friend:

- Your Logo: Reinforces your brand.
- Color Schemes and Fonts: Aligning them with your website builds a cohesive experience for clients.
- "Message to Customer" Box: Great for standard terms or a thank you note.

Line Items: The Meat of It:

- Products/Services: Pull directly from your existing QBO items list for consistency.
- Descriptions: Be clear, but avoid overly technical jargon if your customers aren't experts.
- Quantities, Unit Prices, and Line Totals: Mathematical accuracy is non-negotiable!

Beyond the Basics

- Expiration Date: Sets a deadline and prompts customer follow-up if needed.
- Discounts: Can be itemized or an overall total at the bottom.
- File Attachments: Great for blueprints, project mockups, etc.

QBO's Approval Magic

- Email Directly: Estimate goes out with a trackable link for the client.
- Customer Portal: Some QBO plans let clients view and approve estimates right in a secure portal area.
- E-Signatures: Integrations may be available for legally binding approvals.

Converting Estimates to Invoices with Ease

This is where QBO saves you huge amounts of time. Once the estimate is approved:

- **The "Convert" Option:** Instead of retyping everything, QBO usually has a one-click (or with a few minor edits) conversion process.
- **Accuracy Boost:** Pulls exact pricing, products/services from the estimate, minimizing the risks of typos.
- **Change Management:** If anything *did* need to be adjusted in the final work, you can usually edit while converting the estimate.
- **Customer Connection:** Links the invoice back to the original estimate, providing a clear audit trail for both you and the client.

Why Bother with Formal Estimates?

- **Professionalism:** Sets you apart from competitors scribbling quotes on napkins.
- **Prevents Scope Creep:** The detailed, agreed-upon estimate becomes your shield against "Well, I also thought you were going to..." arguments.

- **Planning Power:** See upcoming work in QBO, aiding in staffing and materials purchasing.

Creating Detailed Purchase Orders to Suppliers

A well-crafted PO does more than just tell your vendor what you want to buy. Here's how to maximize their effectiveness within QBO:

- **Vendor Selection:** Choose from your existing QBO vendor list – this pulls in their contact and default payment terms automatically.
- **Items, Quantities, Pricing:**
- Product/Service Accuracy: Avoid confusion with clear descriptions.
- Unit Costs: Ensure they match your negotiated vendor agreements.
- Pull from Existing Inventory: If you've set up inventory items in QBO, they can populate the PO for consistency.
- **Clear PO Number:**
- QBO often auto-generates one, but you can customize it based on your own internal tracking preferences.
- Essential for Reference: Makes it easy to discuss any issues with the vendor.
- **Delivery Expectations**
- Ship-To Address: Verify if it's your standard location or needs to go to a specific job site.
- Expected Date: Helps you plan for receiving and flags potential delays to notify customers if needed.
- **Additional PO Power Features**
- Terms and Conditions Space: Outline your return policy, etc., adding a layer of protection.
- Internal Notes: Track the reason for the purchase or link it to specific jobs or customers.

- Attachments: If the project involves specs, blueprints, etc., add them directly to the PO for the vendor.

Why Detailed POs Are Your Friend

- **Error Reduction:** A clear PO reduces the chance of receiving the wrong materials, quantities, or being overcharged.
- **Receiving Efficiency:** Your warehouse team can quickly check incoming shipments against the corresponding PO in QBO.
- **Vendor Accountability:** In case of disputes, you have clear documentation of what was agreed upon.
- **Project Costing (If Applicable):** POs become part of your job cost tracking, revealing true profitability.

Linking Purchase Orders to Bills for Accuracy

This is where QBO's automation really shines in your payable process. Here's how it works:

1. **Bill Arrives from Vendor:** When you enter the bill in QBO, there's usually an option to link it to an existing open PO.
2. **Data Magic:** QBO compares your bill entry with the PO it's connected to:

- Items: Did the vendor charge for what was actually ordered?
- Quantities: Any discrepancies between what was ordered and what was billed are flagged.
- Pricing: No more surprise price hikes slipping through! You're alerted to changes.

1. **Approval Workflows (in Some Plans)**

- Bill + PO Combo: Managers get a view of what was ordered AND the bill, making approval more informed.

The Benefits of Linking

- **Faster Bill Payment:** Quick verification against the PO means you can confidently pay accurate bills on time.
- **Fraud Prevention:** Ghost invoices (where a vendor bills for things never ordered) are harder to pull off when POs are in the mix.
- **Audit Happiness:** Organized POs and their corresponding bills demonstrate sound financial practices.
- **Inventory Updates:** QBO's "Receive Against PO" feature automatically increases your inventory quantities when the order arrives and is marked as received.

Pro Tips

- **Partial Shipments:** QBO can handle them! You mark what arrived on a PO, with the remaining quantity still open.
- **Change Orders:** If things need to be modified *after* the PO is sent, adjust the PO in QBO. This keeps accurate records for reference later.
- **PO Reporting:** QBO likely has reports showing your open POs, spend by the vendor, etc. Use these to negotiate better deals.

19

Tracking Customer Projects (Plus or Advanced plans)

P roject tracking in QBO transforms how you manage jobs, ensuring they stay profitable and customers are delighted. Think of it as setting up a mini accounting system within each project for granular visibility.

Setting Up Projects for Clear Job Costing

Let's break down the key elements of starting a new project in QBO:

- **Project "File" Creation:**
- Find the Hub: QBO has a "Projects" tab or similar dedicated area
- New Project Button: Pretty self-explanatory! Look for this to initiate the process.
- **The Essential Info**
- Project Name: Make it descriptive (ex: "Smith Kitchen Remodel")
- Customer Link: Connect the project to the correct customer record in QBO

- Start/End Dates: Optional, but help with planning and reporting
- Project Notes: Capture overall scope, budget, or anything unique about the job
- **Income Tracking Setup:**
- QBO often provides options at this stage:
- Track Income Only: For smaller projects where detailed expense costing isn't as crucial.
- Track Income & Expenses: Enables true job profitability analysis.
- **Customization is Key (Sometimes):**
- QBO might let you add custom fields to the project setup, tailoring it to your specific business.

Why Set Up Projects Diligently?

- **Avoid "Profit Surprises" (Usually Bad Ones):** Knowing if you're truly making money MID-project saves you from a rude awakening at the end.
- **Smarter Resource Allocation:** If a project is bleeding costs unexpectedly, you might be able to adjust staffing or change material suppliers earlier.
- **Customer Communication:** Some QBO plans let you give clients access to project progress info within a portal, increasing transparency.

Tracking Project Income and Expenses

This is where you see whether the budget you quoted is aligned with reality. QBO gives you tools to record both money in and money out against a specific project:

- **Income Side**

- Invoices the Same, But…: When creating an invoice, you'll now have the option to assign it to that project.
- Progress Invoicing Support: For milestone-based billing, QBO can handle that within the project context.
- **Expense Side**
- Bills: Similar to invoices – you link the vendor bill to the project.
- Direct Expenses: If you used a company credit card to buy project supplies, that expense record gets assigned to the project.
- Time Tracking Tie-In: Employee hours logged against a project can automatically be factored into your project cost analysis (payroll setup in QBO is required for this power move).

Project Reporting: Your Crystal Ball

QBO's reports become incredibly powerful once you have project data:

- **Individual Job Profitability:** See at a glance which projects are your cash cows…and which are money pits.
- **By Customer:** Analyze which clients are most profitable to serve – informs your sales strategy.
- **Expense Breakdowns:** Spot if certain material costs are spiraling out of control or a specific subcontractor is consistently over budget.

Pro Tips

- **Project Numbering:** Develop a consistent numbering scheme to easily reference jobs (customer initials, date, etc.)
- **Change Orders Live Here:** Modify the project budget and scope directly within QBO to handle unexpected client requests.
- **Phase/Task Tracking:** Some QBO plans let you break projects

into smaller chunks for even finer-grained cost control.

Monitoring Project Progress and Time Tracking

Beyond financial figures, QBO offers ways to gauge how your projects are doing in terms of the actual work and staying on schedule. Here's how:

- **Project Status Updates**
- Simple Drop down: QBO likely lets you mark a project as "In Progress," "On Hold," "Completed," etc.
- Custom Statuses: Some plans may allow you to create your own to match your workflow.
- **Percentage Complete Field**
- Subjective, But Useful: It's your best guess as to how far along the project is. QBO might use this in reports.
- **Notes for Progress Tracking**
- Free Form Field: Jot down milestones met, challenges encountered, or any updates relevant to the project's status.
- **Time Tracking Integration**
- Requires Payroll Setup: If you use QBO for payroll, employees can often log hours directly to specific projects.
- Manual Time Entry: If you track time outside of QBO, there might be ways to import that data to connect it with the project.
- Costing Power: Those time entries get converted to a dollar figure based on employee pay rates, feeding into your profitability analysis.

Why Track Progress & Time?

- **Spot Bottlenecks Early:** A project stuck at 20% complete for weeks is a red flag to investigate.

- **Client Updates:** Factual statements like "Framing Phase is 50% complete" are better than vague reassurances.
- **Realistic Future Estimates:** If a similar project last month took way longer than quoted, adjust your bids accordingly.
- **Employee Accountability (if Using Time Tracking):** Helps identify who your most efficient workers are, or who might need additional training.

Analyzing Project Profitability

This is where all your data comes together! QBO's project reporting reveals the financial health of individual jobs:

- **The Project Profitability Report**
- This report typically shows:
- Income: Invoices linked to the project.
- Expenses: Direct costs, subcontractor bills, and labor (if pulling in time data).
- Profit/Loss: The bottom line, did you make money?
- Drilling Down: Break expenses into categories to pinpoint problem areas.
- **Additional Profitability Insights**
- Profit as % of Income: Helps you compare projects of different sizes.
- Estimated vs. Actual: Did your initial quote hold up, or are you consistently underestimating?
- By Project Manager: If supported, see who's running the most profitable jobs.

Factors Beyond the Numbers
QBO's reports don't tell the whole story. Consider these qualitative

aspects that also impact true profitability:

- **Client Satisfaction:** A nightmare customer, even on a technically "profitable" project, might not be worth repeating.
- **Lessons Learned:** Sometimes you lose money on a job but gain valuable know-how for smoother future projects.
- **Employee Morale:** Was a project so draining it led to burnt-out staff? That hidden cost impacts future work negatively.

Pro Tips

- **Review Projects Regularly:** Don't just wait until the end to see how you did. Mid-project corrections are possible!
- **"Overhead" Tricky Bit:** True job costing should factor in a portion of your overall business expenses... QBO reports alone might not handle this perfectly.
- **Time Tracking = Power, But Setup Takes Effort:** Training employees to log their time accurately is crucial for the data to be meaningful.

V

Payroll Made Easy (If using QuickBooks Payroll)

20

Setting Up Payroll

S uccessfully navigating the initial configuration will lay a solid foundation for accurate and streamlined payroll processing.

This phase involves building the framework for all your future payroll runs. Here's where the focus will be:

Getting Started: Your Payroll Activation Guide

This guide will vary slightly depending on whether you're a brand-new QuickBooks user or adding payroll to an existing account. Here's the general flow of what you can expect:

Activating Payroll:

- Within QBO: Look for sections prominently labeled "Payroll" or "Employees."
- Selecting a Plan: QuickBooks offers different payroll subscription tiers. Choose the one featuring the level of automation and support

you need.

- Guided Walk through: QBO aims to simplify the process with clear steps tailored to your business.

Gather Your "Know Your Business" Essentials

- Employer Identification Number (EIN): This is your company's tax ID. Absolutely mandatory!
- State Tax IDs: Each state where you have employees might require its own ID number for payroll taxes.
- Bank Account: For both direct deposit of employee paychecks (if offered) and to withdraw tax payments.

Federal and State Tax Forms

- W-4 "On boarding": While technically employee paperwork, QBO ties into the data needed here.
- State-Specific: QBO should guide you on any additional state-level tax forms necessary for your setup.

Existing Payroll Data (If Not Starting From Scratch)

- Year-To-Date Totals: Especially important mid-year, QBO needs accurate figures to avoid over/underpaying taxes.
- Old Paystubs: Good reference point when verifying things are configured correctly.

Key Setup Decisions

Beyond the basic data entry, these choices influence how payroll functions within QuickBooks:

- **Pay Schedules:** Weekly, Bi-Weekly, Monthly...: QBO will likely have these pre-defined, you just select which is right for your employees.
- **Payroll Calculation Method:** Simplified: QuickBooks makes some assumptions for streamlined entry, good for simple salaried employees.
- Detailed: Gives you control over every deduction, bonus type, etc. More complex setup, but necessary for certain pay structures.
- **Automated Tax Setup vs. Do-It-Yourself:** Automation Advantage: QuickBooks can file and pay some of your payroll taxes. Less hassle, but might come with additional fees.
- **Manual Mode:** You still get tax calculations from QBO, but YOU handle the actual filing and payment process. Finer control, but more responsibility on your shoulders.

Pro Tips

- **Don't Rush It:** Payroll mistakes have expensive consequences. Take your time and double-check everything.
- **Help is Available:** QBO Support: They have articles, videos, and likely live chat/phone support to assist with getting payroll configured.
- **Your Accountant:** Involve them early, ESPECIALLY if you have complex pay scenarios (commissions, employees in multiple states, etc.)
- **Test Run Power:** Before processing your first real payroll, do a "dummy" run. This lets you see if the results look right without putting actual money on the line.

Why a Solid Setup Matters

- **Happy Employees Paid on Time** = **Happy You:** Accuracy in payroll is non-negotiable.
- **IRS Doesn't Like Surprises:** Correct configuration is key to avoiding penalties and stressful audits.
- **Informed Decisions:** Well-set-up payroll becomes the source for labor cost reporting – a powerful tool in your business arsenal.

Let's continue our deep dive into the essential setup components for smooth payroll processing with QuickBooks. We'll focus on the crucial company information needed for those tax filings and how to properly configure pay schedules and deductions.

Essential Company Information for Tax Filing

Here's the type of information QBO will likely need from you in order to handle all those behind-the-scenes tax calculations and filings:

Legal Business Name & Address:

- Pull from Official Docs: This must match your tax filings exactly.
- Impacts Reporting: Shows up on employee pay stubs and government forms.

The ID Trifecta

- EIN (Employer Identification Number): Your unique tax identifier obtained from the IRS.
- State Tax ID(s): Required for any state where you have employees.
- Local Tax IDs: Some cities/counties have their OWN tax requirements on top of state and federal.

Company Bank Account Details

- Direct Deposit: If offering this to employees, you need secure bank account info.
- Tax Withdrawal: Even if not using QBO's automated tax service, they often need the account on file to generate reports with the amounts due.

State Unemployment Insurance (SUI) Setup

- SUI Rate: Each state assigns a rate, impacting your payroll tax burden.
- Account Number: You get this when registering with your state's unemployment department.

Worker's Compensation Insurance

- Policy Coverage: QBO may ask if you have it, as it sometimes interacts with payroll calculations.
- Carrier and Rates: Some states require specific data on your policy to be entered for accurate filings.

Why Getting This Right is Critical

- **IRS Penalties are No Joke:** Payroll tax errors can result in hefty fees and fines that eat into your profits.
- **Employee Trust:** Incorrect withholding amounts on their paychecks can cause trouble for *them* come tax season.
- **Reporting Woes:** Without accurate company tax data in QBO, the payroll reports won't be useful.

Configuring Pay Schedules and Deductions

These settings define the rhythm of your payroll process and dictate the amounts that appear on your employees' paychecks. Let's break it down:

Pay Schedules

- Common Options: Weekly, bi-weekly, semi-monthly, monthly. QBO will have these built-in.
- Match Your Reality: Don't pick "bi-weekly" if you ACTUALLY pay every other Friday... even slight variations can throw things off over time.

Deduction Types - The "Less Fun" Part of Pay

- Pre-Tax vs. Post-Tax: This impacts taxable income. QBO helps here, but an accountant's guidance is often wise.
- Federal/State Withholding: Calculated based on employee's W-4 and state equivalents.
- 401k/Retirement: If offered, set the contribution amounts here (either percentage or fixed dollar per paycheck).
- Garnishments: Dealing with court-ordered wage withholding? There's usually a dedicated setup area.
- Additional Deductions: Insurance premiums, company loans, etc., – QBO should be flexible enough to handle them.

Tips for Success

- **Written Policies are Your Friend:** Documenting how often you pay and your standard deductions protects you if there's ever an employee dispute.

- **Automate Where Possible:** QBO aims to calculate taxes once you've set everything up. Less room for manual entry errors!

- **Review, Review, Review:** Before that first payroll, look closely at sample pay stub outputs QBO generates. Catch errors now, not in real life.

21

Adding Employees

The process should be streamlined, but the level of hand-holding from QBO might vary based on your payroll subscription tier. Here's the typical flow:

1. **Dedicated Employee Section:** Look for areas of QBO labeled "Employees," "Payroll," or "Team."
2. **The "Add Employee" Button:** Clearly labeled, this initiates the setup process for each person.
3. **Basic Personal Info:**

- Name (As it must appear on tax forms)
- Address: Impacts local tax calculations, if applicable
- Social Security Number: The linchpin of payroll taxes and reporting
- Contact Info: Optional, but useful for sending pay stub notifications

1. **Pay Settings**

- Pay Type: Hourly vs. Salary – determines how you enter their time

- Pay Rate/Salary Amount: The base figure before any taxes or deductions
- Hire Date: Important for year-to-date calculations for tax forms.

Gathering Employee Data for Accurate Paychecks

Think of this as supplying the ingredients for QBO to cook up a perfectly calculated paycheck. The star of the show is usually:

The Form W-4

- Employee Responsibility: They fill out this federal tax form with filing status and allowances.
- You Keep It On File: Don't send the W-4 to the IRS. QBO translates it into withholding amounts.
- Changes Allowed: Employees can update their W-4 anytime their life situation warrants a change (marriage, having a child, etc.).

State-Specific Withholding Forms

- Similar to W-4: But with rules tailored to your state's income tax laws.
- State Website Source: Your state's department of revenue usually has these forms downloadable.

Direct Deposit Authorization (If Offering It)

- Secure Form: Employee provides their bank account and routing numbers.
- Verify, Verify: A typo here means their paycheck goes into the void! Often a "micro-deposit" test is done.

Deduction Choices

- Health Insurance: If multiple plan options, the employee specifies their choice and any contribution amount.
- 401k (If Offered): Their selected contribution amount (often a percentage of their paycheck).
- Other Voluntary Stuff: Company-specific deductions like uniform costs, parking fees, etc., would be communicated by the employee.

Employee Data Best Practices

- **Privacy Matters:** Payroll data is sensitive. Ensure your QBO setup has appropriate security levels and access is limited to those who truly need it.
- **Paper Backup Isn't Evil:** Even in a digital world, having a file (physical or secure cloud storage) with copies of employee forms protects you if a QBO glitch occurs.
- **Updates as They Happen:** Employees move, get raises, change their withholding... QBO needs to be kept updated to ensure accuracy.

Why Fussing Over Employee Data is Worth It

- **Employee Trust:** Incorrect paychecks erode confidence in you as an employer, even if it was just an innocent data entry error.
- **Smoother Tax Filings:** Those year-end W-2 forms and quarterly reports should practically generate themselves if you've diligently entered employee data.
- **Audit Shield:** Organized records of employee tax forms demonstrate you're doing payroll by the book.

Let's explore ways to streamline employee data collection and the pros and cons of offering direct deposit versus those tried-and-true paper checks.

Self-Service Portals (If Supported) to Streamline On boarding

Some QuickBooks Payroll subscriptions offer a feature that can greatly reduce your administrative workload with new hires. Here's how it works:

- **The Magic Link:** Instead of YOU manually entering all their data, QBO generates a secure link to send the employee.
- **They Do the Work:** The employee accesses a guided portal to submit:
- Basic Personal Info: Name, address, ASSN, etc.
- Electronic W-4 & State Forms: QBO can often store these on file.
- Direct Deposit: They securely provide their own bank account details.
- **You Review & Approve:** It's not completely hands-off! You get to check for any obvious errors before the data is finalized in your payroll system.

Benefits of Self-Service On boarding

- **Less Data Entry for You = Less Chance of Typos:** Reduces the risk of those pesky payroll mistakes that are a pain to unwind.
- **On boarding Anywhere:** Employees aren't tied to doing this only when physically at your office.

- **Digital Docs:** If QBO stores those tax forms for you, it's one less thing to manage in paper files (or worry about losing).
- **Employee Empowerment:** Gives them a sense of ownership over their payroll data right from the start.

Not All Plans Offer This

Be sure to check your specific QuickBooks Payroll features. The more basic tiers might lack this time-saving tool.

Direct Deposit vs. Paper Checks: Understanding the Options

The way money actually flows out of your business and into your employee's hands is a key decision. Let's weigh the options:

Direct Deposit

- **Employee Convenience:** Funds arrive automatically on payday... no trips to the bank to cash a check.
- **Reduced Admin Hassle:** For you, no physical check printing, signing, and distribution.
- **Security Boost:** Eliminates the risk of lost or stolen checks.
- **Potential Fees:** Your bank or payroll provider might charge per-deposit fees.
- **Not for Everyone:** Some employees truly don't have bank accounts, or are resistant to the idea.

Paper Checks

- **Old Reliable:** If you've been doing payroll for ages, this system is familiar.

- **No Tech Required:** Ideal for employees who aren't comfortable with online systems or those with limited bank access.
- **Cost of Supplies:** Blank check stock, printer ink, and secure storage all have a cost.
- **Time Suck:** From the actual printing to distribution, it's less efficient than direct deposit.
- **Security Risk:** Lost/stolen checks are a hassle for everyone, and potential fraud liability for you.

The Hybrid Approach

You CAN mix and match these within QuickBooks. Some employees get direct deposit, others get paper checks – perfectly fine!

Additional Considerations

- **State Laws:** A few states have rules around whether you can MANDATE direct deposit.
- **Reversing Mistakes:** Direct deposit errors can usually be fixed, but it takes a few days, potentially leaving an employee cash-strapped.
- **Payroll Provider Matters:** Some specialize in making direct deposit super smooth, even offering integration with pay card options for unbaked employees.

22

Calculating and Processing Payroll

W e'll cover how to track hours, provide methods for getting that data into QuickBooks, and the importance of a thorough review before hitting "process."

Think of this as the moment when your neatly organized setup meets real-world work hours to generate the all-important numbers for payday.

Entering Hours or Importing Time sheets

How this step looks depends on the nature of your employees and your chosen QuickBooks Payroll features:

Salaried Employees: Simplest Case

- Often No Action Required: If they get paid the same amount regardless of hours worked, QBO just uses their defined salary figure.

Hourly Employees: Manual Entry

- Within QBO: Usually a grid-like form to enter hours each day for each employee
- "Time Clock" Features: Some QBO plans offer a basic digital punch-in/punch-out system employees can access.
- Not Ideal for Complexity: Overtime, multiple pay rates, etc., get cumbersome with manual entry.

Timesheet Import: The Efficiency Booster

- External System: If you use separate software or a dedicated time-tracking tool, QBO likely integrates for easy pulling of data.
- Spreadsheet Upload: If your time sheets are simpler, QBO might allow a template-based upload to streamline the process.

Why Time sheet Accuracy Matters

- **Overpaying Erodes Profits:** Those "extra 15 minutes here and there" backtracked add up to real money over time.
- **Underpaying = Angry Employees:** People are VERY sensitive about short paychecks, damaging morale and trust.
- **Labor Cost Analysis:** If your time sheets tie back to jobs/projects, accurate data is key for knowing true profitability.

Reviewing and Approving Payroll: Your Accuracy Check

Never let payroll run on autopilot! A final review is your chance to catch costly mistakes. QBO helps by:

- **Preview Function:**Before Processing: You should see a summary of each employee's paycheck – gross pay, deductions, net pay.

- Look for Outliers: Does anyone's total seem way too high, or too low? That warrants deeper investigation.
- **Side-by-Side Comparisons (If Available):**Current vs. Prior Pay run: Spotting unexpected jumps or drops in pay for an employee flags a potential data entry error.
- **Payroll Reports:** QBO offers various ways to slice and dice the totals (by department, job, etc.). These are your "sanity check."

Approval Workflows (In Some Plans)

- **Larger Teams:** You might set up a process where a manager reviews payroll BEFORE you finalize it.
- **Audit Trail:** QBO logs who approved it and when – good for accountability and if you ever need to revisit a past pay run.

Processing Day: The Point of No Return (Mostly)

- **Paychecks Generated:** Whether direct deposits sent electronically or physical checks printed depends on your setup.
- **Taxes Calculated & Withheld:** QBO does the heavy lifting, factoring in all those federal, state, and local rules.
- **Reports Updated:** QBO's suite of payroll reports now reflects the freshly processed pay run data.
- **Reversals Are Possible...But Painful:** If you spot a major error AFTER processing, most payroll services allow reversal, but it creates a chain reaction of headaches. Hence the emphasis on pre-processing review!

Absolutely! Let's demystify the automated tax calculations within QuickBooks Payroll and dive into the mechanics of how those pay-checks (physical or digital) actually get into your employee's hands.

Automated Tax Calculations

Here's a simplified view of what's happening behind the scenes:

Data is Power: Based on your company setup (tax IDs, etc.) and each employee's W-4 and state forms, QBO knows the applicable tax rules.

Every Paycheck = Mini Tax Return:

- Gross Pay: Starting point, before any deductions
- Pre-Tax Deductions: 401k contributions, some insurance premiums, etc., reduce taxable income.
- Federal Withholding: QBO applies those complex tables based on the employee's W-4
- State Withholding: Repeat the process, but with your specific state's income tax rules.
- Other Taxes: FICA (Social Security & Medicare), local taxes if applicable… QBO should handle them all..

Employer-Side Taxes Too!

- Don't Forget: You usually pay a portion of Social Security/Medicare, maybe state unemployment tax, etc. These get factored in.

Reports: Your Friend In Case of Audit

- Detailed Breakdown: QBO should offer reports showing EXACTLY how much was withheld for each tax type, both for the employee and your employer-side burden.

Why Automation Isn't Perfect

- **Complex Situations Can Trip It Up:** Multiple jobs for an employee, unusual pre-tax fringe benefits...sometimes manual adjustments are needed.
- **"Up to Date" Is Key:** When tax laws change, QBO updates, but that takes time. Be aware, especially right after major tax legislation passes.
- **It Doesn't File & Pay FOR You (Always):** More on this in the next section!

Generating Paychecks or Initiating Direct Deposits

Payday is what the whole process is about! QBO offers various levels of automation depending on your subscription plan:

DIY Paychecks

- Report to Print: QBO provides the net pay amount, you're still on the hook for check writing, signing, and distribution
- Supplies Needed: Compatible check stock, your printer better work, and be prepared to sign until you get hand cramps.

Partner Power (Add-On Fees Likely)

- Full Service: Some payroll providers partnering with QBO offer check printing AND mailing. Truly hands-off for you.

Direct Deposit: The Most Automated

- Bank File: If you opted for manual tax filing but still want to offer direct deposit, QBO may generate a file to upload to your bank.
- One Click Magic: The higher-tier payroll plans often send the funds

electronically AND handle tax filings – less for *you* to do.

Things to Consider

- **Cost vs. Convenience:** Those add-on services for checks or full-service payroll are tempting, but factor the fees into your decision.
- **Payday Laws:** Each state has rules around how quickly employees must be paid after the pay period ends. QBO won't enforce that for you!
- **Garnishment Handling:** If you're dealing with court-ordered wage garnishments, those add a layer of complexity. Make sure QBO (or your chosen add-on payroll provider) supports them.

23

Filing Payroll Taxes

A bsolutely! Let's navigate the world of payroll tax filings, where QuickBooks can act as your guide (though not always your chauffeur, depending on your subscription level).

The government wants its share of those payroll dollars, and deadlines are non-negotiable. Here's the general flow of federal (and similar processes at the state level):

The Forms:

- Form 941: Quarterly, this is where most federal payroll tax amounts are summarized and reported to the IRS.
- Form 940: Annually, this reconciles your unemployment tax liability (FUTA).
- W-2s: End of year, one copy of these goes to each employee and relevant tax agencies.

Payments Due:

- Not Just Filing: Usually, you also must send in the tax amounts withheld from employee checks ALONG with your employer-side tax burden.
- Frequency Varies: Based on the size of your payroll tax liability, you might pay monthly or semi-weekly.

State = Repeat the Above, But Different:

- Each state has its own versions of tax forms, payment systems, and deadlines.

QuickBooks as Your Tax Filing Assistant

How much assistance varies depending on your QuickBooks Payroll plan. Let's look at the spectrum:

DIY, But Kinda Guided

- Reports are Key: QBO can generate the detailed tax reports with the raw dollar amounts you'll need to fill out the forms yourself.
- Deadlines: It might alert you to upcoming due dates, but ultimately, you're responsible for not missing them.
- Manual Filing & Payments: You're logging into IRS (and state) websites to submit the forms and send money separately.

Automated Filing...Maybe Paying Too

- E-Filing Integration: Some QuickBooks Payroll plans directly connect to the IRS and/or state systems for electronic filing.
- Payment Pull: The highest-tier plans might automatically withdraw tax funds from your bank account on the due date and pay the

government on your behalf.

- Check Those Fees: This convenience often comes with additional fees on top of your base payroll subscription.

Why Filing Correctly and On Time Matters

- **IRS Penalties are STEEP:** Late filings, underpayment, etc., trigger fines that snowball quickly and can jeopardize your business.
- **State Tax Agencies: Can Be Even Nastier:** Don't underestimate the power of your state department of revenue to make your life difficult.
- **Employee W-2s: Also Have Deadlines:** Providing correct W-2s on time avoids issues for your employees when THEY file their personal tax returns.

Situations Where QBO Isn't a Perfect Tax Solution

- **Household Payroll ("Nanny Tax"):** QBO may not handle specific forms required for domestic workers.
- **Highly Customized Scenarios:** Complex deductions or multiple state filings sometimes exceed QBO's native capabilities.
- **Behind on Filings:** QBO doesn't magically fix a pre-existing mess. In these cases, get an accountant involved ASAP.

Additional Considerations

- **EFTPS is Your Friend (and Enemy):** This is the IRS's Electronic Federal Tax Payment System. Even if not using QBO's automated pay, you'll likely need to use EFTPS.
- **State Systems Vary Wildly:** Some are modern, others feel like stepping into a time machine back to 1998.

- **"Backup Plan" Mentality:** Even if you automate filings, understanding the reports QBO generates is smart. If their system glitches, it's on YOU to catch the problem.

Automated vs. Manual Payroll Tax Filing: Choosing What Fits You

The decision boils down to a trade-off between absolute control and saving your precious time. Here's how to weigh your options:

Automated Tax Filing

- **The Allure:** Set it and (mostly) forget it. QBO handles submitting forms and (potentially) paying the taxes for you.
- **Ideal For:**
- Truly Time-Strapped: If the thought of another form fills you with dread, automation is appealing.
- Simple Payroll: The more standard your pay scenarios, the more likely QBO can handle things accurately.
- "Peace of Mind" Factor: Reducing the chance of human error lessens that tax-season anxiety.
- **The Downsides:**
- Cost: Automated tax services nearly always come with additional fees.
- Less Control: You're putting blind faith in QBO always being accurate and up-to-date on any tax law changes.
- Troubleshooting: If something goes wrong, you're less equipped to fix it since you're not intimately familiar with the forms.

Manual Tax Filing

- **Full Control:** You're filling in every box on the forms yourself and initiating the payments.
- **Ideal For:**
- Cost Conscious: If your budget is tight, avoiding those extra automation fees might be necessary.
- Complex Payroll: Unique benefit scenarios or employees working in multiple states can warrant manual oversight.
- Tax-Savvy Folks: If you or someone on your team actually enjoys the puzzle of tax forms, DIY makes sense.
- **The Downsides**
- Time Investment: It takes longer, plain and simple. More room for data entry mistakes too.
- Requires Knowledge: You need to understand the instructions for those tax forms and keep up on any filing changes.
- Deadline Pressure: YOU are fully responsible for not missing those payment and filing due dates.

The Hybrid Approach

- **QBO Reports As Your Base:** Even if you manually file, QBO's detailed payroll tax reports give you the necessary raw numbers.
- **Automate Some, Not All:** Perhaps you e-file at the federal level, but handle your state taxes manually, for example.

Understanding Tax Deadlines and Penalties

Ignoring deadlines is like playing with fire when it comes to payroll taxes. Here's why you should become intimately familiar with them:

They Vary!

- Deposit Schedule: Monthly or semi-weekly, depends on your payroll tax liability size.
- Quarterly Forms: Form 941 is the biggie here.
- Annual Filings: Form 940 and employee W-2s kick in at year-end.
- State Differences: Each state has its own set of deadlines on top of the federal ones.

IRS Penalty Structure

- Late Filing: Percentage of the tax due, increasing the longer you wait.
- Late Payment: Even if you file on time but pay late, penalties still apply.
- Interest: On top of penalties, they charge interest...because of course they do.
- Extreme Cases: Repeated noncompliance can lead to criminal charges and even your business being shut down.

States Can Be Even Harsher: Don't assume they'll mirror the IRS penalty structure.

Where to Find Deadlines

- **IRS Website (The Source):** https://www.irs.gov/ has publications outlining due dates.

State Department of Revenue Website: Each has its own online resources.

24

QuickBooks Payroll 2024 Updates

W hile we can't predict the future with absolute certainty, we can identify key areas to keep a watchful eye on as 2024 goes on. Important note: QuickBooks usually rolls out updates throughout the year, not just one big bang update.

Changes to Tax Rates and Filing Requirements

Payroll taxes are one of the least stable things in business. Be prepared for adjustments like these:

Income Tax Withholding Tables:

- Federal: The IRS often tweaks the amounts withheld based on tax brackets and standard deduction changes.
- State: Your state may adjust its own withholding tables, especially if major tax legislation passed.

Social Security & Medicare (FICA):

- Taxable Wage Base: The maximum amount of earnings subject to Social Security tax sometimes increases, impacting both employees and your employer-side liability.
- Rates Less Likely: The actual tax rates for FICA change less often, but it's not impossible.

Unemployment Taxes

- SUTA Rates: State unemployment tax rates are assigned to each business based on their claims history. Yours could fluctuate year to year.
- Federal (FUTA): The rules around these tax credits evolve, potentially impacting your bottom line.

Local Taxes: Don't underestimate the power of cities and counties. New payroll taxes or sudden enforcement of existing ones can throw a wrench into the works.

New Filing Deadlines: While rare, major tax overhauls sometimes come with shifts in when forms and payments are due.

How QuickBooks Handles Change

QuickBooks aims to shield you from having to become a tax law expert. Here's how they typically respond to changes:

- **Software Updates:** These are pushed out (sometimes automatically) that include new tax tables, updated form layouts, etc.
- **In-App Notifications:** QBO often displays alerts when major updates impact your payroll process.
- **Knowledge Base and Support:** Their help articles are kept up-to-date and they likely offer live support if you're confused by a

change.

Why Staying Informed Matters

- **Avoiding Nasty Surprises:** Finding out you've been underpaying taxes mid-year leads to penalties and interest.
- **Employee Trust:** Incorrect withholding amounts on paychecks can mess with *their* tax situation at year-end, damaging morale.
- **Budgeting Power:** If your payroll tax burden increases, that needs to be factored into your financial planning.

Staying Informed: Resources for the Latest Payroll Updates

Don't wait for QuickBooks to tell you everything! Be proactive with these resources:

- **IRS Website** (https://www.irs.gov/): Newsroom section covers important tax law changes.
- **Your State Department of Revenue:** Their website should have business-focused tax updates.
- **Payroll Provider Blogs:** Companies specializing in payroll often maintain blogs explaining changes in plain English.
- **Your Accountant:** Especially for major tax overhauls, their guidance is invaluable for navigating how it impacts your specific business.

Additional 2024 Possibilities

Beyond tax specifics, here's where QBO Payroll might evolve in other ways:

- **Enhanced Automation:** Streamlining more of the tax filing/payment process for supported scenarios.

- **Integrations:** Partnering with HR platforms or benefit providers to create a more seamless employee management experience.
- **Reporting & Analytics:** More robust payroll data reporting tools to aid in workforce-related financial decisions.

New or Expanded Payroll Features in QuickBooks

While we can't definitively predict QuickBooks' development road map, considering industry trends and user wish lists can give us clues about what new features might emerge:

Enhanced On boarding Tools

- Self-Service Deep Dive: Guiding employees through tax forms with clear explanations specific to their state, not just the generic form.
- I-9 Integration: Streamlining the Form I-9 (employment eligibility verification) process, including potential e-signature options.
- Direct Deposit Evolution: Partnering with more financial institutions for same-day or early access to paychecks for employees.

Compensation Flexibility

- Beyond Hourly/Salary: Easier tracking of complex commission scenarios, bonus calculations, and flexible pay periods.
- PTO Accrual & Liability: Built-in tools to manage various paid time off policies and automatically calculate the financial liability on your balance sheet.
- "Expense" Reimbursements: Smoother handling of employee reimbursements and the ability to mark those payments as non-taxable to the employee.

Focus on Compliance

- Multi-State Magic: QBO gets better at handling employees working in states different from your business's home base.
- "What If" Tax Calculators: Model the impact of hiring in new states or making significant pay changes *before* doing them.
- Audit Prep: Centralized reporting hub making it dead simple to gather exactly what an IRS auditor might want, reducing stress.

Niche Industry Support

- Tip Handling: Intuit already has solutions for restaurants, expanding this within QBO would be logical.
- Clergy-Specific Rules: Payroll for churches has unique tax wrinkles, QBO could build out dedicated features.
- Contractor (1099) Tie-In: Smoother tracking of 1099 payments alongside W-2 payroll to catch potential misclassification issues.

Staying Informed: Resources for the Latest Payroll Updates

Knowledge is power when it comes to navigating the ever-changing world of payroll! Here's where to stay ahead of the curve:

- **QuickBooks Blog & Social Media:**
- Product Announcements: They often highlight new payroll features here.
- Follow Them: Twitter, etc., can provide quick updates between major blog posts.
- **Webinars and Training Resources**
- QBO Hosted: They often run sessions on "What's New in Payroll" after major updates.
- Third-Party Experts: Accounting firms specializing in QuickBooks sometimes offer more targeted payroll training.
- **In-App Notifications**
- Don't Ignore: QBO puts alerts within the software when changes impact you. Actually read them!
- The "What's New" Section: Some QBO plans have a dedicated area summarizing recent updates.
- **Payroll Community Forums**
- User-to-User Help: Other business owners often spot changes or clever workarounds before official QBO support channels address them.
- Intuit Lurks: Sometimes QuickBooks employees monitor the forums, giving hints about future development.
- **Your Payroll Service Provider (If Using One)**
- Their Job to Know: A good payroll provider should proactively notify you of changes impacting your account setup.

Pro Tips

- **Accountant Is Your Ally:** They often have broader industry insights and can spot if a QBO update is out of sync with tax law realities.

- **Seasonal Vigilance:** Be extra aware at year-end (W-2 time) and when new tax laws take effect, as this often triggers QBO changes.

VI

Understanding Sales Tax

25

Setting Up Sales Tax

Taxes, the unavoidable part of running a business, often feel like navigating a labyrinth. Sales tax, in particular, can be a confusing maze with its intricate rules and varying rates.

This sub chapter will equip you with the knowledge and tools to confidently configure sales tax in your QuickBooks Online account. We'll delve into the fundamentals, explore the automated features, and address common scenarios, ensuring you emerge from the sales tax labyrinth victorious.

Before we delve into the intricacies of sales tax configuration, let's ensure we're starting on solid ground. Here is what to consider:

Business Location: Your business address determines which tax agencies you'll need to file with and the applicable sales tax rates.

Nexus: This refers to your physical presence in a state, which triggers sales tax collection obligations.

Taxable Items: Identify the products and services subject to sales tax in your jurisdiction.

Real-Life Example: Let's say you own a bakery in California. Most baked goods are taxable, but certain items like fresh produce might be exempt.

Exempt Customers: Certain customers, like non-profit organizations, may be exempt from sales tax.

With these foundational elements in place, let's explore the automated features QuickBooks Online offers to streamline sales tax setup.

Automating the Maze: Leveraging QuickBooks Online's Power

QuickBooks Online understands the complexities of sales tax and provides a user-friendly, automated setup process. Here's how it works:

- Navigate to Taxes > Sales Tax.
- Click "Get Started."
- Verify your business address. This automatically identifies the relevant tax agencies.
- Select your filing frequency based on your estimated sales tax liability.
- Choose whether you want to collect sales tax (most businesses do).
- Review and confirm the settings.

With these steps, QuickBooks Online automatically calculates sales tax on your invoices and tracks your sales tax liability. It's like having a friendly Ariadne guiding you through the labyrinth, ensuring you don't get lost in the tax maze.

Customizing Sales Tax Settings

While the automated setup is incredibly helpful, there are situations where customization might be necessary. Let's venture into some common scenarios:

- Multiple Tax Rates: If your business operates in multiple locations with varying sales tax rates, you can configure QuickBooks Online to apply the correct rate based on the customer's location.
- Real-Life Example: Imagine you have an online store selling nationwide. You'll need to set up different tax rates for each state where you have nexus.
- Tax-Exempt Customers: You can create tax-exempt customer profiles to ensure sales tax isn't applied to their transactions.
- Real-Life Example: A non-profit organization purchasing supplies for a charity event would be exempt from sales tax.
- Overriding Automatic Calculations: In rare instances, you might need to manually override the calculated sales tax amount. This can be done directly on invoices or in the Sales Tax Center.

Remember, even with the automated features, it's crucial to stay informed about sales tax regulations in your specific jurisdiction. Consulting with a tax advisor is always recommended for complex situations or specific industry-related tax rules.

Advanced Maneuvers

While the basics are essential, QuickBooks Online offers additional functionalities to streamline sales tax management:

- Tax Reports: Utilize various sales tax reports to analyze your sales tax liability, identify trends, and prepare for tax filings.
- Real-Life Example: The "Sales Tax Liability by Customer" report helps you understand which customers contribute most to your sales tax burden.
- Tax Groups: Create tax groups to assign specific tax rates to different categories of products or services, simplifying tax calculations.
- Real-Life Example: You could create a tax group for "Prepared Foods" with a 9% tax rate and another group for "Beverages" with a 0% rate.
- Automation Rules: Set up automation rules to automatically apply specific tax rates or exemptions based on predefined criteria.
- Real-Life Example: You could create a rule to automatically exempt all sales to customers with a valid tax-exempt certificate.

By understanding these advanced features, you can further optimize your sales tax management within QuickBooks Online.

Peace of Mind with QuickBooks Online

By following these steps and understanding the key concepts, you've successfully navigated the sales tax labyrinth with QuickBooks Online as your guide. You can now confidently manage sales tax within your business, ensuring accurate calculations, timely filings, and peace of mind.

Remember, QuickBooks Online is constantly evolving, offering new features and updates to simplify tax management.

26

Automated Sales Tax Calculations (Plus or Advanced plans)

I magine the stress of manually calculating sales tax fading into a distant memory. Picture the hours saved by eliminating the need to research complex rates, exemptions, and filing deadlines. With QuickBooks Online's automated sales tax feature, this dream becomes a reality.

This subchapter is your personal guide to navigating the automated sales tax landscape within QuickBooks Online. We'll delve into the intricacies of this powerful tool, ensuring you become a master of sales tax calculations in no time.

Understanding Automated Sales Tax

Think of automated sales tax as your own personal tax wizard. It takes the burden of manual calculations off your shoulders, ensuring accuracy and saving you precious time. Here's how it works:

QUICKBOOKS ONLINE 2024 BEGINNER'S GUIDE

- Location, Location, Location: The system uses your business address and customer locations to determine the applicable tax rates. No more scrambling through tax tables or memorizing complex formulas.
- Tax Rate Magic: QuickBooks Online automatically updates your tax rates based on the latest regulations, eliminating the risk of outdated calculations.
- Exemption Efficiency: Identify tax-exempt customers and apply the appropriate rules with ease, ensuring you only collect what's necessary.
- Filing Made Simple: Generate sales tax reports with a few clicks, streamlining the filing process and reducing the chances of errors.

Embarking on the Automated Journey: Setting Up Your System

Before we dive into the nitty-gritty, let's get your system configured for automated sales tax:

- Company Address: Ensure your business address is accurate within QuickBooks Online. This forms the foundation for all tax calculations.
- Sales Locations: Specify whether you sell within or outside your home state. This helps the system determine the appropriate tax jurisdictions.
- Tax Agencies: Add the relevant tax agencies you collect sales tax for, including details like filing frequency and start dates.
- Tax Items: Create tax items for each tax agency, specifying the rates and any applicable rules.

Managing Tax Items

Tax items are the building blocks of automated sales tax. Here's how to manage them effectively:

- Tax Rate Setup: Enter the tax rates for each tax agency, ensuring they align with current regulations.
- Taxable Items: Specify which products and services are subject to sales tax. This helps the system apply the correct rates automatically.
- Tax Rules: Configure rules for specific situations, like tax-exempt products or reduced rates for certain locations.
- Real-Life Example: Let's say you own a bakery selling online across multiple states. With automated sales tax, you don't need to worry about applying different rates for each state. QuickBooks Online automatically calculates the correct tax based on the customer's shipping address, ensuring compliance and eliminating the risk of errors.

Creating Transactions

Now that your system is primed, let's explore how automated sales tax works in action:

- Customer Information: Ensure your customer addresses are accurate and complete. This is crucial for applying the correct tax rates.
- Sales Transactions: When creating invoices or sales receipts, the system automatically calculates sales tax based on the customer's location and the taxable items included.
- Review and Edit: You can always review the calculated tax and make manual adjustments if needed.

- Real-Life Example: Imagine you have a customer in California who places an order for cookies. QuickBooks Online will automatically apply the 7.25% state sales tax to the invoice, ensuring accurate calculations and compliance.

Understanding Sales Tax Reports

QuickBooks Online provides comprehensive sales tax reports, offering valuable insights:

- Sales Tax Liability: Track the total sales tax you owe to each tax agency, ensuring timely payments.
- Sales Tax Activity: Analyze sales tax collected and paid over specific periods, providing valuable financial data.
- Tax Detail Reports: Drill down into individual transactions to understand the tax breakdown for each sale.

Reconciling for Accuracy: Ensuring Peace of Mind

While automated sales tax streamlines the process, reconciliation remains crucial. Regularly compare your sales tax reports with the amounts you've paid to the tax agencies. This ensures accuracy and identifies any potential discrepancies that require further investigation.

Integration Power: Leveraging the Full Potential

QuickBooks Online integrates seamlessly with other features, further enhancing your sales tax management. For instance, inventory tracking allows you to automatically calculate tax on the cost of goods sold, providing a more accurate picture of your tax liability. Additionally, expense tracking can help you identify and claim tax-deductible expenses related to sales tax payments.

Overcoming Common Hurdles

Even with automated sales tax, occasional errors might arise. Here are some troubleshooting tips:

- Incorrect Tax Rates: Double-check your tax items and ensure they reflect the latest rates.
- Customer Address Errors: Verify that customer addresses are accurate and complete, as this directly impacts tax calculations.
- Taxable vs. Non-Taxable Items: Review your product and service categories to ensure they are correctly classified as taxable or non-taxable.

By embracing the power of automated sales tax in QuickBooks Online, you've unlocked a world of efficiency and accuracy. Remember, consistent review and occasional manual adjustments are crucial, but the system handles the heavy lifting, freeing you to focus on what truly matters – running your business. So, go forth and conquer the sales tax maze with confidence, knowing that QuickBooks Online is your trusty guide on this journey.

27

Filing Sales Tax Returns

R emember the days of manually calculating sales tax, poring over spreadsheets, and wrestling with filing deadlines? Well, those days are over. With QuickBooks Online, filing sales tax returns becomes a streamlined and stress-free process. This sub chapter equips you with the knowledge and tools to navigate the world of sales tax returns with confidence.

Think of QuickBooks Online as your personal tax filing assistant. It meticulously tracks your sales tax throughout the year, calculates the amounts owed, and guides you through the filing process with ease. This sub chapter delves into the intricacies of filing sales tax returns within QuickBooks Online, ensuring you meet your tax obligations efficiently and accurately.

Understanding the Basics

Before diving into the filing process, let's establish some key concepts:

- Filing Frequency: This refers to how often you need to file your sales tax returns, determined by your state or local tax agency. It can be monthly, quarterly, or annually.

- Tax Agencies: Identify the specific tax agencies you collect sales tax for, like your state's Department of Revenue.
- Tax Periods: Each filing period represents a specific time frame for which you'll file a return. QuickBooks Online automatically calculates the dates based on your filing frequency.
- Real-Life Example: Let's say you own a small clothing boutique in Texas with a quarterly filing frequency. This means you need to file sales tax returns for every three-month period (January-March, April-June, etc.). QuickBooks Online will automatically track your sales and tax liability within these quarters, making the filing process more manageable.

Embarking on the Filing Journey: Step-by-Step Guide

Now, let's explore the actual process of filing sales tax returns in QuickBooks Online:

- Navigate to the Sales Tax Center: Locate the "Taxes" section within QuickBooks Online and select "Sales Tax." This opens the Sales Tax Center, your hub for all sales tax-related activities.
- Identify the Return to File: Under the "Filings" tab, you'll see a list of upcoming and past sales tax returns. Select the return you need to file based on the current tax period.
- Review and Adjust: QuickBooks Online automatically populates the return with details like gross sales, taxable sales, and calculated tax owed. You can review these figures and make adjustments if necessary.
- Real-Life Example: During your review, you might notice that

179

a specific sale was incorrectly categorized as non-taxable. You can easily rectify this by editing the transaction and ensuring it's classified as taxable within QuickBooks Online.

- Finalize and Submit: Once satisfied with the information, click "File Now." QuickBooks Online generates the return, which you can then submit electronically to the relevant tax agency (e-filing options vary by agency).

Beyond the Basics: Additional Considerations

While the core filing process is straightforward, here are some additional points to consider:

- Tax Payments: Record your sales tax payments within QuickBooks Online after filing the return. This ensures accurate tracking and reconciles your accounts.
- Taxable vs. Non-Taxable Items: Double-check that your products and services are categorized correctly as taxable or non-taxable to avoid discrepancies in your return.
- Tax-Exempt Customers: Ensure accurate customer information, including tax-exempt status, to avoid collecting unnecessary sales tax.
- Real-Life Example: You have a non-profit organization registered as a customer. By marking them as tax-exempt within QuickBooks Online, the system automatically excludes them from sales tax calculations, ensuring compliance.

Common Filing Errors and Troubleshooting:

Even with QuickBooks Online's assistance, mistakes can happen. Here are some common filing errors and how to address them:

- Incorrect Tax Rates: Ensure your tax items are configured with the current tax rates for each jurisdiction you collect sales tax in. If you notice discrepancies, update the rates immediately and recalculate the affected returns.
- Missing Information: Missing customer information or product categorization can lead to inaccurate calculations. Double-check your data and ensure all relevant details are complete.
- Late Filings: Penalties and interest accrue for late filings. Set calendar reminders and prioritize timely submissions to avoid unnecessary financial repercussions.

Advanced Filing Features:

QuickBooks Online offers advanced functionalities to streamline the filing process:

- Sales Tax Reports by Location or Product: Generate detailed reports to analyze sales tax collected by specific locations or product categories. This provides valuable insights for tax planning and business strategy.
- Automated Filing Reminders: Set up automated email notifications to remind you about upcoming filing deadlines, ensuring you never miss a submission.
- Integration with Other Tools:

QuickBooks Online integrates seamlessly with other accounting software or tax preparation tools. This can save time by automatically importing data and generating reports, further simplifying the filing process.

Reconciling for Accuracy: Ensuring Peace of Mind

After filing your return and recording the payment, it's crucial to reconcile your sales tax accounts. Compare the amounts reported on your return with the actual tax payments made to the tax agency. This helps identify any discrepancies and ensures your records are accurate.

VII

Generating Financial Reports

.

28

The Importance of Financial Reports

I magine navigating a dark forest without a compass. That's essentially running a business without understanding your financial reports. These reports are your business's vision tracker, revealing its past, present, and even hinting at its future financial health. In this chapter, we'll delve into the significance of financial reports and how QuickBooks Online makes accessing and interpreting them a breeze.

Let's break it down:

- **Understanding Your Financial Performance:** Financial reports paint a clear picture of your business's financial performance. You'll see how much money you're making (revenue), how much you're spending (expenses), and what your overall profit or loss is. This knowledge is crucial for making informed business decisions, like pricing your products or services competitively or identifying areas to cut costs.

- **Tracking Your Financial Health:** Think of your financial reports as a health check for your business. They reveal your assets (what you own), liabilities (what you owe), and equity (the difference between the two). This information helps you assess your financial stability, identify potential risks, and make strategic plans for growth.

- **Meeting Tax Requirements:** Filing your taxes accurately and on time is vital for any business. Financial reports provide the necessary data to prepare your tax returns, ensuring you comply with tax regulations and avoid penalties.
- **Securing Funding and Investments:** Need a loan or attract investors? Financial reports demonstrate your business's financial viability and potential for success. They act as a powerful tool to convince lenders and investors that your business is a worthwhile investment.

Now, let's explore the three key financial reports generated by Quick-Books Online:

1. **Profit and Loss Statement (P&L):** This report summarizes your business's income and expenses over a specific period. It essentially tells you whether you're making a profit or incurring a loss. Imagine you run a clothing boutique. Your P&L will show how much revenue you generated from selling clothes and accessories, how much you spent on inventory and rent, and ultimately, your overall profit.

P&L in Action:

Let's say your P&L reveals that your summer clothing line is a massive hit, but your winter collection isn't selling as well. This insight allows you to adjust your inventory purchases for the upcoming season, focusing on items with higher demand. Additionally, you might consider offering discounts or promotions on your winter clothing to boost sales and maximize your overall profit margin. The P&L is your road map to profitability, and QuickBooks Online makes analyzing it a breeze. You can easily identify trends, pinpoint areas for improvement, and make data-driven decisions to optimize your boutique's financial performance.

1. **Balance Sheet:** This report offers an overview of the financial situation of your company at a particular moment in time. It shows your assets (cash, inventory, equipment), liabilities (loans, accounts payable), and equity (the difference between the two). Think of it as a financial photograph of your clothing boutique at the end of the month. It reveals how much cash you have on hand, how much you owe to suppliers, and the overall value of your business.

Balance Sheet: Your Financial Snapshot:

Your balance sheet might show that you have a significant amount of inventory on hand, but your cash reserves are low. This could indicate that your inventory turnover rate is slow, meaning your products are taking longer to sell. To address this, you might implement strategies like offering faster shipping options or running targeted promotions to encourage quicker sales and improve your cash flow. By regularly reviewing your balance sheet, you can assess your financial stability. If your liabilities are significantly higher than your assets, it might indicate potential financial strain. This prompts you to take corrective actions like securing additional funding or reducing expenses to ensure a healthy balance between your assets and liabilities.

1. **Cash Flow Statement:** This report monitors the flow of money into and out of your company. It shows how much cash you received from sales, how much you paid for expenses, and any

changes in your cash balance over time. This is particularly important for businesses like yours, where managing cash flow is crucial.

Cash Flow: The Lifeblood of Your Business:

Imagine your cash flow statement shows that your expenses are consistently exceeding your income, resulting in a negative cash flow. This can lead to difficulties meeting your financial obligations and hinder your boutique's growth. By analyzing your cash flow statement, you can proactively manage your finances. You might consider negotiating better payment terms with your suppliers, delaying non-essential expenses, or exploring alternative financing options to ensure you have enough cash on hand to cover your expenses and avoid potential financial hiccups.

Remember, QuickBooks Online makes generating and understanding these reports incredibly simple. You can access them anytime, anywhere, empowering you to make informed financial decisions that drive your boutique's success.

With these financial reports as your guiding light, you'll be able to navigate the financial landscape of your business with confidence, making informed decisions that lead to long-term prosperity.

29

Profit and Loss Statement

Imagine steering a ship without a compass. Sure, you might reach land eventually, but navigating the vast ocean without direction is risky and inefficient. Similarly, running a business without understanding your Profit and Loss (P&L) statement is like sailing blind. This crucial financial report acts as your business's financial compass, revealing its overall financial health and guiding you towards profitability.

In this sub-chapter, we'll delve into the world of P&L statements and how QuickBooks Online makes generating and interpreting them a breeze. Buckle up, as we navigate the key elements of this essential financial report:

- **Understanding the Basics:** A P&L statement summarizes your business's income and expenses over a specific period, typically a month, quarter, or year. It essentially tells you whether you're making a profit (yay!) or incurring a loss (uh oh!). Think of it like a detailed record of your business's financial activity. On one side, you have all the money coming in from sales (your revenue). On the other side, you have all the money going out for expenses (rent, salaries, and supplies). The difference between these two amounts is your net profit or loss, the ultimate indicator of your business's financial well-being.

Real-Life Example: Let's say you run a dog walking service. Your P&L statement might show that you generated $5,000 in revenue from dog walking sessions last month. However, you also spent $1,000 on gas, $500 on dog treats and supplies, and $800 on insurance. In this scenario, your net profit would be $2,700 ($5,000 - $1,000 - $500 - $800).

- **Beyond the Bottom Line:** While the net profit is the headline, the P&L offers valuable insights beyond just a single number. By analyzing the individual income and expense categories, you can identify areas where your business excels and areas that need improvement. For example, your P&L might reveal that your morning walks are consistently booked, but your afternoon slots remain open. This information allows you to adjust your pricing or marketing strategies to attract more clients during the afternoon, ultimately maximizing your revenue potential.
- **QuickBooks Online to the Rescue:** Manually generating P&L statements can be time-consuming and error-prone. Thankfully, QuickBooks Online automates this process, providing you with clear and accurate P&L reports anytime, anywhere. You can easily customize the time frame, compare results across different periods, and even drill down into specific income and expense categories for a deeper analysis.

Understanding your P&L statement is like having a financial road map for your business. It empowers you to make informed decisions about:

```
Pricing: Are you charging enough to cover your expenses and
generate a profit?
Staffing: Do you need to hire additional staff or can you
optimize your current team's workload?
Inventory: Are you stocking the right amount of supplies to
meet customer demand without incurring unnecessary costs?
Marketing: Are your marketing efforts generating enough leads
and sales to justify the investment?
```

By utilizing the insights provided by your P&L statement, you can make strategic adjustments that drive your business towards financial success. Remember, QuickBooks Online is your co-pilot on this journey, making it easier than ever to navigate the financial landscape and ensure your business thrives.

30

Balance Sheet

I magine taking a snapshot of your home. That picture captures its current state, revealing the furniture, decorations, and overall atmosphere. Similarly, a Balance Sheet is a financial snapshot of your business at a specific point in time, offering a clear picture of its financial health and stability.

In this sub-chapter, we'll delve into the key components of a Balance Sheet and how QuickBooks Online makes generating and understanding it a breeze. Let's navigate the three crucial elements that make up this essential financial report:

- **Understanding the Basics:** The Balance Sheet provides a clear picture of what your business owns (assets), what it owes (liabilities), and the difference between the two, which represents your business's net worth or equity. Think of it as a financial equation: Assets - Liabilities = Equity. Assets are anything your business owns that holds value, like cash in the bank, inventory on hand, or equipment you use to operate. Liabilities represent your business's debts, such as outstanding loans, unpaid bills, or wages owed to employees. Equity is essentially what's left after you subtract your liabilities from your assets.

Real-Life Example: Let's say you run a clothing boutique. Your Balance Sheet might show that you have $10,000 in cash in the bank, $5,000 worth of clothing inventory, and a $20,000 loan you recently took out to expand your store. On the other side, you might have $2,000 owed to suppliers and $1,000 in unpaid rent. In this scenario, your assets total $35,000, your liabilities total $3,000, and your equity (net worth) is $32,000.

Beyond the Snapshot: While the Balance Sheet offers a valuable snapshot, its true power lies in the insights it provides beyond the surface level. By analyzing the individual asset and liability categories, you can:

- **Assess Financial Stability:** A healthy balance sheet typically shows assets exceeding liabilities, indicating your business has enough resources to cover its debts. Conversely, if your liabilities are significantly higher than your assets, it might signal potential financial strain.
- **Identify Potential Risks:** A high amount of inventory compared to cash might indicate slow sales, potentially leading to cash flow issues. Similarly, a large amount of debt could restrict your ability to invest in growth opportunities.
- **Track Progress Over Time:** Comparing your Balance Sheets over different periods allows you to monitor your business's financial growth or decline. Are your assets increasing steadily? Are you effectively managing your liabilities?
- **Benchmark Your Performance:** Comparing your Balance Sheet to industry benchmarks or your own historical data can reveal areas where your business excels or needs improvement. For instance,

a higher inventory turnover ratio compared to your competitors might indicate more efficient inventory management practices.

- **QuickBooks Online: Your Balance Sheet Navigator:** Quick-Books Online makes generating and analyzing Balance Sheets effortless. You can access them in real-time, allowing you to monitor your financial position throughout the year. Additionally, you can easily categorize your assets and liabilities, track their changes over time, and even generate comparative reports to assess your financial progress against industry standards or your own historical performance. This level of detail and accessibility empowers you to make informed decisions that drive your business towards long-term financial success.

Don't forget, the Balance Sheet is not just a financial report; it's a powerful tool for understanding your business's financial standing and making strategic decisions that ensure its stability and growth. With QuickBooks Online as your guide, you can interpret your Balance Sheet with confidence and use its insights to navigate your business towards a prosperous future.

31

Cash Flow Statement

I magine a river. The water flowing through it represents the cash flowing in and out of your business. While the overall water level might seem stable, understanding the flow itself is crucial. That's where the Cash Flow Statement comes in, acting as your business's financial lifeline, revealing how efficiently your cash is moving.

In this sub-chapter, we'll delve into the intricacies of the Cash Flow Statement and how QuickBooks Online makes generating and interpreting it a breeze. Let's navigate the three key sections that track the lifeblood of your business:

- **Understanding the Basics:** The Cash Flow Statement tracks the movement of cash in and out of your business over a specific period, typically a month, quarter, or year. It essentially tells you where your cash comes from (cash inflows) and where it goes (cash outflows). This information is vital for understanding your business's financial health and liquidity. Think of it like a detailed record of your cash transactions. Cash inflows might include sales revenue, loan proceeds, or investments. Cash outflows could be expenses like rent, salaries, inventory purchases, or loan repayments. By analyzing the difference between these inflows and outflows, you gain valuable insights into your cash flow situation.

Real-Life Example: Let's say you run a consulting firm. Your Cash Flow Statement might show that you generated $10,000 in revenue from client projects last month. However, you also paid $5,000 in salaries, $2,000 in office rent, and $1,000 for software subscriptions. In this scenario, your net cash flow would be $2,000 ($10,000 - $5,000 - $2,000 - $1,000).

Beyond the Bottom Line: While the net cash flow is important, the Cash Flow Statement offers a deeper analysis by categorizing your cash activities into three sections:

- **Operating Activities:** This section tracks cash generated from your core business operations, such as sales of goods or services, payments to suppliers, and employee wages. Analyzing this section reveals your business's ability to generate cash through its core activities.
- **Investing Activities:** This section tracks cash inflows and outflows related to investments, like purchasing equipment or selling assets. Understanding this section helps you assess how your investment decisions impact your cash flow.
- **Financing Activities:** This section tracks cash inflows and outflows related to financing your business, such as loan proceeds, repayments, or issuing stock. Analyzing this section reveals how you're managing your debt and equity financing.

By understanding these categories, you can identify potential cash flow bottlenecks, areas for improvement, and opportunities to optimize your financial health.

- **QuickBooks Online: Your Cash Flow Navigator:** QuickBooks Online makes generating and analyzing Cash Flow Statements effortless. You can access them in real-time, allowing you to monitor your cash flow situation throughout the month or quarter. Additionally, you can customize the time frame, compare results across different periods, and even drill down into specific cash flow categories for a more granular analysis.

Keep in mind, a healthy cash flow is the lifeblood of your business. By utilizing the insights provided by the Cash Flow Statement and leveraging the user-friendly features of QuickBooks Online, you can ensure your business has the financial resources needed to thrive. With this knowledge, you'll be able to make informed decisions about managing your cash flow, optimizing your operations, and securing a prosperous future for your business.

32

Other Essential Reports

While the Profit and Loss, Balance Sheet, and Cash Flow Statement are the financial reporting cornerstones, QuickBooks Online offers a treasure trove of other valuable reports that can provide deeper insights into your business's performance. Think of them as specialized tools that shed light on specific aspects of your financial operations, empowering you to make informed decisions and optimize your business for success.

In this sub-chapter, we'll delve into some of these essential reports and how they can benefit your business:

- **Accounts Receivable Aging:** Imagine forgetting who owes you money and when. The Accounts Receivable Aging report acts as your memory bank, providing a detailed breakdown of your outstanding customer invoices categorized by their age (how long they've been overdue). This information is crucial for managing your collections process effectively, ensuring timely payments and minimizing cash flow disruptions.
- **Accounts Payable Aging:** Just like you have customers who owe you, you also have vendors you owe money to. The Accounts

Payable Aging report tracks your outstanding bills categorized by their due date. This helps you prioritize payments, avoid late fees, and maintain strong relationships with your vendors.

- **Sales by Customer/Product/Service:** Understanding which customers, products, or services generate the most revenue is vital for making informed business decisions. These reports provide detailed breakdowns of your sales, revealing your top performers and areas that might require adjustments in your marketing or product offerings.
- **Inventory Valuation:** For businesses that carry physical inventory, knowing its value is crucial. The Inventory Valuation report provides a snapshot of your on-hand inventory, categorized by item, cost, and total value. This helps you optimize your inventory levels, avoid overstocking, and ensure you have enough product to meet customer demand.
- **Budget vs. Actual:** Budgeting is essential for financial planning, but how do you know how well you're sticking to your plan? The Budget vs. Actual report compares your budgeted income and expenses to your actual results, highlighting any variances. This allows you to identify areas where you're exceeding or falling short of expectations and make adjustments to your budget or business operations as needed.
- **Customizable Reports:** The beauty of QuickBooks Online lies in its flexibility. Custom reports can be made to meet your unique requirements. For example, you might want to track sales by location, analyze profitability by project, or monitor specific expense categories. This level of customization empowers you to gain deeper insights into specific aspects of your business and make data-driven decisions that drive growth.

Remember, these reports are not just numbers on a page; they are powerful tools for understanding your business's financial health, identifying areas for improvement, and making strategic decisions that propel you towards success. With QuickBooks Online as your guide, you can unlock the full potential of these reports and gain a comprehensive understanding of your financial landscape.

33

Customizing Reports

While the pre-built reports in QuickBooks Online offer valuable insights, the true magic lies in its customization capabilities. Think of it like a chef's kitchen – you have the ingredients (data), but the ability to personalize them into a dish that perfectly suits your taste buds (business needs) is what makes the experience truly unique and satisfying.

In this sub-chapter, we'll delve into the exciting world of customizing reports in QuickBooks Online and how it can empower you to gain deeper understanding of your business:

- **Tailoring Reports to Specific Needs:** Imagine you are in need of a report that tracks sales by product category and location. While QuickBooks Online might not have this specific report pre-built, you can easily create one by selecting the relevant data fields (product category, location, sales amount) and customizing the layout to display the information in a way that best suits your analysis. This level of flexibility allows you to extract the exact information you need to make informed decisions.
- **Analyzing Trends and Identifying Patterns:** By customizing

reports to focus on specific time frames or group data by relevant criteria, you can uncover hidden trends and patterns that might not be readily apparent in standard reports. For example, a custom report grouping expenses by department might reveal that one department is consistently exceeding its budget, prompting further investigation and potential cost-saving measures.

- **Monitoring Key Performance Indicators (KPIs):** Every business has specific metrics that define its success. By creating custom reports that track these KPIs, you can easily monitor your progress and identify areas that require improvement. For instance, a restaurant owner might create a report tracking average customer spend per visit, allowing them to analyze the effectiveness of their marketing campaigns and pricing strategies.

- **Visualizing Data for Enhanced Understanding:** QuickBooks Online allows you to transform your data into visually appealing charts and graphs. This makes complex information easier to digest and identify patterns or trends at a glance. Imagine a pie chart showing the breakdown of your expenses by category, instantly revealing which areas consume the most resources.

- **Sharing Insights with Stakeholders:** Once you've created a customized report that provides valuable insights, you can easily share it with key stakeholders like investors, partners, or management teams. This promotes transparency and ensures everyone is on the same page regarding your business's financial performance.

Don't forget, customization is not just about making reports look fancy; it's about extracting the most relevant and actionable information from your data. With QuickBooks Online as your guide, you can unlock the full potential of report customization and gain a deeper understanding of your business's unique financial landscape, ultimately driving informed decisions and propelling your business towards success.

Beyond the Basics: Ease and Accessibility

The beauty of QuickBooks Online lies in its user-friendly approach to report customization. Here's what makes it accessible even for those without extensive accounting experience:

- **Intuitive Interface and User-Friendly Features:** QuickBooks Online's interface is designed for ease of use. Selecting data fields, adjusting filters, and customizing layouts are all done through simple clicks and drags, eliminating the need for complex coding or technical knowledge. This empowers you to take control of your financial information without relying solely on accounting professionals.
- **Saving Custom Reports for Future Use:** Once you've created a customized report that perfectly suits your needs, you can save it for future reference. This eliminates the need to rebuild the report each time you want to analyze the same data, saving you valuable time and effort.
- **Sharing Templates and Collaborating with Others:** Quick-Books Online allows you to share your customized report templates with colleagues or your accountant. This fosters collaboration and ensures everyone has access to the same information, promoting transparency and streamlined financial analysis within your business.

Do mind that, report customization is not a one-time event; it's an ongoing process of refining your understanding of your business and extracting the most relevant insights from your financial data. With QuickBooks Online as your guide, you can transform your financial data into actionable intelligence that drives your business towards success.

VIII

Advanced Features and Integrations

34

Budgeting Tools

Think of navigating a ship without a map. While you might have a general direction in mind, the chances of reaching your destination safely and efficiently are slim. Budgeting in business is no different. Without a clear financial road map, achieving your goals can be a perilous journey.

This is where QuickBooks Online's powerful budgeting tools come in. Think of them as your compass and anchor, guiding you towards financial stability and success. Here these tools and how they can empower you to take control of your business's financial future:

- **Creating a Budget:** QuickBooks Online makes creating budgets a breeze. You can choose between Profit & Loss and Balance Sheet budgets, depending on your needs. Simply select the desired time frame (yearly, quarterly, or monthly) and start entering your projected income and expenses for each relevant account. This process is intuitive and user-friendly, even for those with limited accounting experience.

Real-Life Example: Let's say you run a bakery. You might create *a Profit & Loss budget, estimating your projected sales revenue from different product categories and factoring in your expected costs for ingredients, rent, salaries, and utilities. This budget becomes your financial road map for the year, allowing you to track your progress and make adjustments as needed.*

- **Subdividing and Customizing:** QuickBooks Online goes beyond basic budgeting. You can subdivide your budgets by location, department, or any other relevant criteria. This allows for granular analysis and pinpoints areas where you might need to adjust your spending or marketing efforts for specific segments of your business.

- **Scenario Planning:** What if you want to test different financial scenarios? QuickBooks Online allows you to create multiple budget versions, simulating potential outcomes based on different sales forecasts, expense adjustments, or economic conditions. This proactive approach helps you prepare for unexpected circumstances and make informed decisions that mitigate potential risks.

- **Budget vs. Actual Reports:** The true power of budgeting lies in comparing your projections to reality. QuickBooks Online's Budget vs. Actuals report reveals any discrepancies between your planned and actual income and expenses. This invaluable information allows you to identify areas where you're exceeding or falling short of your goals, prompting adjustments to your budget or business operations as needed.

- **Monitoring Progress and Making Adjustments:** Budgeting is an ongoing process, not a one-time event. Regularly reviewing your Budget vs. Actuals reports allows you to monitor your progress, identify trends, and make adjustments to your budget or business strategies throughout the year. This ensures you stay on track towards achieving your financial objectives.

Recall to mind, budgeting is not just about creating numbers on a page; it's about gaining control over your financial future. By effectively utilizing QuickBooks Online's budgeting tools, you can:

- Set realistic and achievable financial goals.
- Make informed decisions about resource allocation.
- Identify potential cash flow issues and proactively address them.
- Measure your progress and adapt your strategies as needed.
- Increase your business's overall financial stability and success.

Beyond the Basics: Optimizing Your Budget Journey

With QuickBooks Online as your guide, you can transform budgeting from a tedious task into a strategic tool that empowers you to navigate the financial landscape with confidence and achieve long-term prosperity. Here's how:

- **Identifying Cost-Saving Opportunities:** By regularly reviewing your Budget vs. Actuals reports, you might discover areas where you're consistently exceeding your planned expenses. This could lead to identifying unnecessary spending or negotiating better deals with vendors, ultimately saving your business valuable resources. For example, you might discover that a specific supplier charges higher prices than competitors, prompting you to seek alternative options.
- **Adapting to Changing Market Conditions:** The business landscape is dynamic. By monitoring your budget progress, you can identify situations where your actual results deviate significantly from your initial projections. This might be due to unexpected market trends, changes in customer behavior, or unforeseen circumstances like material shortages or economic downturns.

209

Recognizing these deviations allows you to adapt your budget and business strategies accordingly, ensuring your financial plan remains relevant and achievable. For instance, a sudden surge in demand for a specific product might necessitate increasing production capacity and adjusting your budget for inventory and equipment purchases.

• **Motivating and Empowering Your Team:** Sharing your budget with your team and tracking progress together fosters a sense of ownership and accountability. Seeing how their actions impact the overall financial picture can motivate employees to make responsible decisions and contribute to the company's financial success. For example, sharing sales targets with your sales team and tracking progress against budget can incentivize them to achieve their goals and contribute to the company's overall revenue growth.

Don't forget, budgeting is a continuous journey of learning and adaptation. With QuickBooks Online as your guide, you can leverage its powerful tools to gain valuable insights, make informed decisions, and ultimately steer your business towards a prosperous future.

35

Project Tracking & Profitability (Plus or Advanced plans)

I magine juggling multiple projects simultaneously. Keeping track of income, expenses, and profitability for each one can be a daunting task. Thankfully, QuickBooks Online Plus and Advanced plans offer a powerful solution: Project Tracking and Profitability.

In this sub-chapter, we'll explore how these features empower you to:

- **Streamline Project Management:** Easily create and manage individual projects within QuickBooks Online. Assign customers, track income and expenses, and monitor progress – all from a centralized dashboard. This eliminates the need for spreadsheets or separate project management tools, saving you time and effort.

  Real-Life Example: Let's say you run a marketing agency. You can create separate projects for each client campaign, tracking income from invoices, expenses like advertising costs and employee salaries, and the overall profitability of each project. This allows you to identify which campaigns are generating the most revenue and optimize your strategies accordingly.

- **Accurate Cost Tracking:** Project tracking meticulously captures all project-related expenses, including materials, labor costs, and overhead. This comprehensive view ensures you have a clear understanding of your true project costs, preventing hidden expenses from eroding your profitability.
- **Automatic Time Tracking Integration:** For businesses using QuickBooks Time, integrating it with project tracking allows automatic syncing of employee hours spent on each project. This eliminates manual time tracking and ensures accurate labor costs are allocated to the appropriate projects.
- **Profitability Reports:** Gain instant insights into your project's financial performance with comprehensive profitability reports. These reports detail total revenue, expenses, and net profit for each project, allowing you to identify the most profitable ventures and areas for improvement.
- **Data-Driven Decision Making:** With project profitability data readily available, you can make informed decisions about resource allocation, pricing strategies, and project selection. This data-driven approach helps you maximize profitability and optimize your overall business operations.

Remember, project tracking and profitability are not just about tracking numbers; they are about gaining strategic insights into your project portfolio. By leveraging these features in QuickBooks Online Plus and Advanced plans, you can:

- Improve project management efficiency.
- Ensure accurate cost tracking and profitability analysis.
- Identify and prioritize high-performing projects.

- Make data-driven choices to maximize the effectiveness of your company plan.
- Ultimately, achieve greater profitability and success.

Unlocking Advanced Features

While the core functionalities of project tracking are valuable, Quick-Books Online Plus and Advanced plans offer additional features that further enhance your project management capabilities:

- **Budgeting and Forecasting:** Set project budgets and track progress against them in real-time. This allows you to identify potential cost overruns early on and take corrective action.
- **Scenario Planning:** Simulate different project scenarios by adjusting budget allocations and resource estimates. This proactive approach helps you prepare for unexpected situations and make informed decisions.
- **Customizable Dashboards:** Tailor your project dashboard to display the most relevant metrics for your specific needs. This personalized view provides a quick snapshot of your project's performance and allows you to focus on the most critical information.
- **Collaboration Tools:** Share project details and reports with team members, clients, or stakeholders. This fosters transparency and streamlines communication, ensuring everyone is on the same page.

Remember, project tracking and profitability are powerful tools that empower you to manage your projects effectively and achieve greater financial success. With QuickBooks Online Plus and Advanced plans as your guide, you can gain valuable insights, make informed decisions, and ultimately drive your business towards long-term profitability.

213

Continuous Improvement and Growth: A Journey, Not a Destination

By consistently analyzing project data and identifying areas for improvement, you can continuously refine your project management processes. This ongoing learning cycle ensures your projects are executed with greater efficiency and profitability over time. Consider these additional aspects:

- **Identifying Bottlenecks:** Project tracking data can reveal bottlenecks that hinder project progress. This could be inefficient workflows, resource constraints, or communication gaps. By identifying these bottlenecks, you can implement solutions to streamline processes and optimize project execution.
- **Benchmarking and Industry Standards:** Compare your project performance against industry benchmarks or internal historical data. This allows you to identify areas where your projects are exceeding or falling short of expectations and implement corrective measures to improve overall project performance.
- **Investing in Project Management Training:** Equipping your team with project management best practices can significantly enhance project execution and profitability. Consider providing training on project planning, resource allocation, and risk management to empower your team to deliver successful projects consistently.

Keep in mind, project tracking and profitability are powerful tools that empower you to manage your projects effectively and achieve greater financial success. This journey of continuous learning and optimization ensures that your project management practices evolve alongside your business, leading to sustainable success in the long run.

36

Time Tracking

Have you tried managing a team without knowing how they spend their time. It's like driving blind – you might reach your desired end eventually, but the journey will be inefficient and potentially costly. Thankfully, QuickBooks Online offers a powerful solution: Time Tracking. Think of it as your digital clock-in system, providing real-time insights into how your team's time is utilized.

In this sub-chapter, we'll explore how QuickBooks Online Time Tracking empowers you to:

- **Streamline Payroll Processing:** Eliminate manual time card calculations and ensure accurate payroll by automatically syncing tracked hours with your payroll system. This saves you time and minimizes the risk of errors.

    Real-Life Example: Say you run a construction company. Your employees track their hours on specific projects using the time clock feature. This data is automatically integrated with your payroll, ensuring accurate pay calculations based on actual working hours for each project.

- **Boost Project Management:** Track time spent on individual projects, allowing you to analyze project efficiency and identify areas for improvement. This data helps you optimize resource allocation and ensure projects stay on track.
- **Invoice Clients Accurately:** Track billable hours for client projects and easily convert them into invoices. This ensures you get paid for the time your team invests in delivering services.
- **Gain Valuable Insights:** Generate comprehensive time tracking reports that reveal employee productivity trends, project profitability, and overall resource utilization. This data empowers you to make data-driven decisions that optimize your business operations.

Do not forget, time tracking is not just about monitoring hours; it's about gaining valuable insights into your team's workflow and optimizing resource allocation. By effectively utilizing QuickBooks Online Time Tracking, you can:

- Reduce administrative burdens and save time.
- Ensure accurate payroll processing and minimize errors.
- Improve project management and resource allocation.
- Invoice clients accurately and efficiently.
- Make data-driven decisions to boost overall business performance.

Time Tracking Features and Customization

While the core functionalities of time tracking are valuable, QuickBooks Online offers additional features that enhance your time management capabilities:

- **Mobile App:** Track time on-the-go with the mobile app, allowing employees to clock in and out from any location. This ensures accurate time tracking even for remote teams.

- **Customizable Workflows:** Set up custom workflows to categorize time entries by project, customer, service type, or any other relevant criteria. This allows for granular analysis and tailored reporting.

- **GPS Location Tracking:** (Optional) Enable GPS location tracking to monitor employee activity and ensure they are working from authorized locations. This can be particularly valuable for field service businesses.

- **Integration with Third-Party Apps:** Integrate QuickBooks Time with other business tools like project management software or expense tracking apps for a seamless workflow.

Remember, time tracking is a powerful tool that empowers you to gain control over your most valuable resource – your team's time. With QuickBooks Online as your guide, you can leverage its features and customization options to:

- Streamline time tracking processes and boost efficiency.
- Gain valuable insights into employee productivity and resource utilization.
- Optimize project management and client billing practices.
- Make data-driven decisions that propel your business towards success.

Continuous Improvement: The Key to Long-Term Efficiency Gains

By regularly analyzing time tracking data and identifying areas where time is underutilized or wasted, you can continuously refine your workflows and optimize your team's efficiency. This ongoing process ensures that your team is consistently working towards achieving your business goals with maximum effectiveness. Consider these additional aspects:

- **Identifying Time-Consuming Tasks:** Time tracking data can reveal tasks that are taking longer than expected. This could indicate inefficient processes, inadequate training, or resource constraints. By identifying these time-consuming tasks, you can implement solutions like process automation, training programs, or resource reallocation to streamline workflows and improve overall efficiency.
- **Employee Feedback and Collaboration:** Encourage open communication with your team and actively seek their feedback on time tracking processes and workflow bottlenecks. This collaborative approach fosters a sense of ownership and empowers employees to suggest improvements that can significantly enhance overall efficiency.
- **Invest in Time Management Training:** Equipping your team with effective time management skills can significantly improve individual productivity and overall team performance. Consider providing training on time management techniques, prioritization strategies, and distraction management to empower your team to utilize their time effectively.

Remember, time tracking is a powerful tool that empowers you to gain control over your most valuable resource – your team's time. With QuickBooks Online as your guide, you can leverage its features and customization options to:

- Streamline time tracking processes and boost efficiency.
- Gain valuable insights into employee productivity and resource utilization.
- Optimize project management and client billing practices.
- Make data-driven decisions that propel your business towards success.
- Continuously improve your workflows and maximize your team's potential.

By effectively utilizing time tracking features and embracing continuous improvement, you can transform your business operations into a well-oiled machine, maximizing efficiency and achieving long-term success.

37

Exploring QuickBooks Online Apps

Tried running a furniture business with just a hammer and screwdriver? While these tools might get the job done, having a full toolbox filled with specialized equipment makes tasks faster, easier, and more efficient. QuickBooks Online Apps are like that toolbox for your financial management. They extend the functionality of your accounting software, allowing you to customize your experience and streamline specific processes.

In this sub-chapter, we'll explore the exciting world of QuickBooks Online Apps and how they can empower you to:

- **Automate Repetitive Tasks:** Simplify tedious, time-consuming tasks like expense tracking, bill payments, and bank reconciliations with specialized apps. This frees up your valuable time to focus on strategic business growth.

    Real-Life Example: Say you own a restaurant. Instead of manually entering every receipt into QuickBooks, you can connect an expense tracking app. This app automatically captures receipt data, categorizes expenses, and imports them directly into your accounting software, saving you significant time and effort.

- **Gain Industry-Specific Insights:** Find apps tailored to your specific industry, providing specialized features and reports that cater to your unique business needs. This targeted functionality helps you make informed decisions based on industry-specific benchmarks and insights.
- **Connect with Essential Tools:** Integrate your favorite business tools and services like CRM platforms, project management software, and e-commerce solutions with QuickBooks Online Apps. This seamless workflow eliminates data silos and streamlines your overall business operations.
- **Boost Efficiency and Productivity:** By automating tasks, leveraging industry-specific tools, and integrating essential services, QuickBooks Online Apps empower you to work smarter, not harder. This translates to increased efficiency, improved productivity, and ultimately, greater profitability.

Remember, QuickBooks Online Apps are not just add-ons; they are strategic extensions that can transform your financial management. By effectively utilizing them, you can:

- Save time and effort by automating repetitive tasks.
- Gain valuable industry-specific insights for better decision-making.
- Connect your favorite business tools for a seamless workflow.
- Boost overall efficiency and productivity for long-term success.

Finding the Perfect Fit: Exploring the App Marketplace

With hundreds of apps available in the QuickBooks Online App Store, finding the right ones can feel overwhelming. Here are some tips:

- **Identify Your Needs:** Start by pinpointing areas where your current workflow feels inefficient or time-consuming. Are you struggling with expense management, inventory tracking, or project collaboration? Identifying your specific needs will help you focus on relevant apps.

- **Read Reviews and Ratings:** Before installing any app, check user reviews and ratings to gauge its functionality, ease of use, and overall user satisfaction. This feedback from fellow QuickBooks Online users can be invaluable in making informed choices.

- **Start with Free Trials:** Many apps offer free trials, allowing you to test their features and compatibility with your workflow before committing. This "try-before-you-buy" approach ensures you choose apps that truly add value to your business operations.

Remember, the beauty of QuickBooks Online Apps lies in their diversity and flexibility. By exploring the App Store and strategically integrating the right tools, you can tailor your accounting software to your unique business needs and achieve optimal efficiency and success.

Building a Powerful Ecosystem with Continuous Improvement

While individual apps offer valuable benefits, the true power lies in building an interconnected ecosystem within QuickBooks Online. Here are some additional considerations for maximizing your app experience:

- **Data Synchronization:** Ensure seamless data flow between your chosen apps and QuickBooks Online. This eliminates the need for manual data entry and ensures consistency across your financial records.

- **Customizable Dashboards:** Utilize the power of app integrations to create personalized dashboards that display key metrics and reports from various tools. This centralized view provides a comprehensive overview of your business performance at a glance.
- **Workflow Automation:** Connect multiple apps to automate complex workflows. For instance, automatically generate invoices upon project completion or trigger expense approvals based on pre-defined criteria. This level of automation streamlines your operations and minimizes manual intervention.
- **Continuous Evolution:** Building a powerful app ecosystem within QuickBooks Online is an ongoing process. As your business evolves and your needs change, you can continuously refine your app portfolio by:
- Exploring new apps that address emerging challenges or opportunities.
- Re-evaluating existing app integrations to ensure they remain relevant and aligned with your evolving workflows.
- Automating additional tasks and workflows to further streamline your operations.

By embracing this continuous improvement mindset, you ensure your QuickBooks Online environment remains dynamic and adaptable, constantly supporting your business growth and success.

Remember, QuickBooks Online Apps are not just individual tools; they are building blocks for a powerful financial management ecosystem. By strategically integrating and customizing your app portfolio, creating a seamless workflow, and embracing continuous improvement, you can create a powerful and efficient financial management system that propels your business towards long-term success.

38

Artificial Intelligence Enhancements in 2024

R emember the days of manually entering every transaction, meticulously categorizing expenses, and wrestling with complex financial reports? Thankfully, those days are fading into the past. Artificial intelligence (AI) is rapidly transforming the accounting landscape, and QuickBooks Online 2024 is at the forefront of this revolution.

In this sub-chapter, we'll explore the exciting AI enhancements coming to QuickBooks Online in 2024 and how they can empower you to:

- **Automate Repetitive Tasks with Unmatched Accuracy:** AI algorithms in QuickBooks Online 2024 are trained to automatically categorize transactions, reconcile bank statements, and even generate reports with incredible precision. This translates to less manual data entry, fewer errors, and more time for you to focus on strategic financial planning.

  Real-Life Example: Imagine never having to manually categorize that stack of receipts again. AI in QuickBooks Online can analyze each receipt, identify the vendor, extract key information like amount and date, and automatically categorize it as the correct expense. This not only saves you time but also minimizes the risk of human error.

- **Gain Personalized Insights and Recommendations:** As AI learns about your business within QuickBooks Online, it can provide tailored insights and recommendations. This could include identifying potential tax deductions you might have missed, reminding you of upcoming deadlines, or even suggesting areas for cost optimization based on your historical data.

- **Enjoy Enhanced Cash Flow Forecasting:** Leveraging historical data and industry trends, AI-powered cash flow forecasting in QuickBooks Online 2024 will provide you with a more accurate and predictive picture of your future financial health. This allows you to make informed decisions about investments, expenses, and resource allocation with greater confidence.

- **Experience a Smarter, More Interactive User Experience:** Get ready for advanced AI-powered chat bots within QuickBooks Online. These chatbots will act as your virtual assistants, guiding you through various processes, answering your questions in real-time, and streamlining your overall user experience.

Keep in mind, AI in QuickBooks Online 2024 is not just about automation; it's about unlocking a new level of financial intelligence and efficiency. By leveraging these advancements, you can:

- Save significant time and effort on tedious tasks.
- Gain valuable insights and recommendations for better decision-making.

- Improve cash flow management and financial forecasting.
- Enjoy a more intuitive and interactive user experience.

Embracing the Future of Accounting with AI

As AI continues to evolve, so too will its capabilities within QuickBooks Online. Here are some additional thoughts on how you can best utilize these advancements:

- **Stay Informed:** Keep yourself updated on the latest AI features and functionalities within QuickBooks Online. As the technology progresses, new features and enhancements will become available, further streamlining your financial management processes.
- **Embrace the Learning Curve:** While AI in QuickBooks Online is designed to be user-friendly, there might be a slight learning curve as you adapt to its capabilities. Don't hesitate to explore the features, experiment with different functionalities, and seek support if needed.
- **Focus on Strategic Tasks:** With AI handling the mundane, you can dedicate your time and energy to the bigger picture. Analyze the insights provided by AI, make strategic financial decisions, and focus on growing your business with confidence.

Keep in mind, AI in QuickBooks Online 2024 is not just a technological upgrade; it's a paradigm shift in how you manage your finances.

IX

Troubleshooting and Getting Help

39

Common Errors and How to Fix Them

E ven the most meticulous bookkeeper can encounter errors in their accounting software. While QuickBooks Online is designed to be user-friendly, glitches and unexpected issues can sometimes arise. Don't panic! This chapter equips you with the knowledge to tackle common QuickBooks Online errors and get your financial data back on track.

Remember, most errors in QuickBooks Online fall into three main categories:

- **Connectivity Issues:** These errors often stem from internet connection problems, firewall settings, or browser compatibility issues.
- **Data Errors:** Inaccurate data entry, missing information, or inconsistencies can lead to errors in calculations, reports, and reconciliations.
- **Software Glitches:** Occasionally, software updates or bugs can cause unexpected behavior within QuickBooks Online.

By understanding these categories and the common errors within them, you can effectively troubleshoot and resolve most issues yourself. Let's delve into some specific examples:

Connectivity Gremlins:

- **Error Message:** "Unable to connect to the company file."
- **Possible Cause:** This error often indicates an internet connection issue.
- **Solution:** Verify you have a stable internet connection. Check your firewall settings to ensure they don't block QuickBooks Online. Try a different browser or clear your browsing cache.

Data Discrepancies:

- **Error Message:** "The balance in your bank statement does not match your account balance."
- **Possible Cause:** This discrepancy usually arises from missing transactions, incorrect categorization, or duplicate entries.
- **Solution:** Carefully review your bank statement and reconcile it with your QuickBooks Online account. Ensure all transactions are entered accurately and categorized correctly. Check for duplicate entries and remove them.

Software Hiccups:

- **Error Message:** "QuickBooks Online has encountered an unexpected error."
- **Possible Cause:** This could be due to a software update glitch or a temporary bug.
- **Solution:** Close and reopen QuickBooks Online. Clear your

browser cache and cookies. If the issue persists, check the Quick-Books Online Help Center for known issues and solutions. You can also contact QuickBooks support for further assistance.

Proactive Troubleshooting Tips

Here are some additional strategies to minimize errors and maintain a smooth workflow in QuickBooks Online:

- **Regular Backups:** Regularly back up your company file to ensure you have a secure copy in case of data loss or software malfunction.
- **Data Validation:** Develop a routine to verify the accuracy of your data entry. This includes double-checking transaction details, categorizations, and bank reconciliations.
- **Software Updates:** Keep QuickBooks Online updated with the latest versions to benefit from bug fixes and performance improvements.
- **Seek Support:** Don't hesitate to utilize the vast resources available from QuickBooks Online, including the Help Center, community forums, and customer support.

Remember, even with the best practices, errors can still occur. By understanding the root causes of these errors and implementing corrective measures, you can not only resolve the immediate issue but also refine your accounting practices for greater accuracy and efficiency in the long run.

Turning Errors into Opportunities for Improvement

While encountering errors in QuickBooks Online can be frustrating, it's important to remember that they often serve as valuable learning opportunities. By understanding the root causes of these errors and implementing corrective measures, you can not only resolve the immediate issue but also refine your accounting practices for greater accuracy and efficiency in the long run.

Think of troubleshooting as an opportunity to strengthen your financial data management skills and build confidence in your ability to navigate the software effectively. With the knowledge and resources provided in this chapter, you are well-equipped to tackle common errors in QuickBooks Online and maintain a healthy financial management system for your business.

40

Using QuickBooks Online Help Resources

Q uickBooks Online is a powerful tool, but even the most seasoned users encounter challenges sometimes. Don't worry, help is readily available! QuickBooks boasts a wealth of resources designed to guide you through any obstacle, ensuring your financial management journey remains smooth and efficient.

This sub-chapter equips you with the knowledge to navigate the vast array of QuickBooks Online help resources, empowering you to:

- **Find Answers Quickly:** Utilize the built-in search function and browse categorized articles to find solutions to specific questions or troubleshooting needs.
- **Connect with Experts:** Access live chat support, phone support, and the QuickBooks Online community forum to receive personalized assistance from knowledgeable professionals and fellow users.
- **Expand Your Knowledge:** Explore educational resources like video tutorials, webinars, and training classes to deepen your understanding of QuickBooks Online functionalities and best practices.

Remember, effectively utilizing these resources transforms you from a user facing a hurdle into a self-sufficient problem-solver, maximizing your QuickBooks Online experience. Let's delve into the specifics:

Mastering the Search Function:

The search bar within QuickBooks Online is your first line of defense. Simply type your question or keyword, and the system will display relevant articles, tutorials, and troubleshooting guides.

> **Real-Life Example:** *Stuck on how to reconcile your bank statement? Type "bank reconciliation" in the search bar. You'll be presented with detailed instructions, step-by-step guides, and troubleshooting tips to get you back on track.*

Connecting with Live Support:

When the search function doesn't quite cut it, QuickBooks Online offers multiple avenues for live support:

- **Chat Support:** Engage in real-time chat with a QuickBooks Online support specialist who can answer your questions and guide you through specific tasks.
- **Phone Support:** Speak directly with a support representative for personalized assistance with complex issues or troubleshooting.
- **Community Forum:** Connect with a vibrant community of QuickBooks Online users and professionals. Share your challenges, learn from others' experiences, and gain valuable insights from fellow entrepreneurs.

Expanding Your Knowledge Base:

QuickBooks Online goes beyond simply resolving immediate issues. It offers a wealth of educational resources to help you master the software and optimize your financial management:

- **Video Tutorials:** Access a vast library of short, informative videos demonstrating specific QuickBooks Online features and functionalities.
- **Webinars:** Attend live or recorded webinars hosted by Quick-Books experts, covering various topics like advanced accounting practices, industry-specific insights, and best practices for financial management.

Building a Self-Reliant Financial Management Journey

You can find quick answers to common questions, connect with experts for personalized assistance, and continuously expand your knowledge base through educational resources.

Remember, mastering these resources transforms QuickBooks Online from a software program into a powerful tool that supports your financial growth and empowers you to make informed business decisions with confidence. So, never hesitate to leverage the wealth of help available and embark on a self-reliant journey towards financial success.

41

Finding a QuickBooks ProAdvisor

As stated earlier QuickBooks Online is a powerful tool, but sometimes navigating its intricacies requires a helping hand. Enter the QuickBooks Pro-Advisor – a certified expert who can provide personalized guidance and support, ensuring your financial management journey remains smooth and successful.

This sub-chapter equips you with the knowledge to:

- **Identify When You Need a Pro-Advisor:** Understand situations where seeking professional assistance can significantly benefit your business.
- **Find the Right Pro-Advisor:** Learn about the resources available to locate a qualified Pro-Advisor who aligns with your specific needs.
- **Build a Collaborative Relationship:** Establish effective communication and collaboration strategies to maximize the value of your Pro-Advisor partnership.

Remember, a Pro-Advisor can become an invaluable asset, offering specialized knowledge and expertise to optimize your QuickBooks Online experience and elevate your financial management practices. Let's delve into the specifics:

Knowing When to Seek Professional Help:

While QuickBooks Online is user-friendly, certain scenarios call for the expertise of a Pro-Advisor:

- **Complex Business Needs:** If your business has intricate financial structures, industry-specific requirements, or complex accounting processes, a Pro-Advisor can provide tailored guidance and ensure compliance with regulations.

  Real-Life Example: Owning a restaurant with multiple locations and inventory management complexities might necessitate a Pro-Advisor's expertise to optimize inventory tracking, payroll processing, and tax reporting within QuickBooks Online.

- **Advanced Features:** Utilizing advanced features like inventory management, payroll processing, or job costing can be more efficient with the assistance of a Pro-Advisor who can configure and optimize these functionalities for your specific needs.

  Real-Life Example: Implementing project costing for a construction company requires in-depth knowledge of the feature and its integration with other aspects of QuickBooks Online. A Pro-Advisor can ensure accurate project tracking and reporting.

- **Troubleshooting Complex Issues:** When encountering persistent errors or challenges beyond your troubleshooting skills, a Pro-

Advisor can provide in-depth analysis and solutions to get your financial data back on track.

Real-Life Example: Repeated bank reconciliation discrepancies or complex error messages might indicate deeper issues within your QuickBooks Online setup. A Pro-Advisor can diagnose the root cause and implement corrective measures.

Finding the Perfect Pro-Advisor Fit:

QuickBooks offers various resources to locate a Pro-Advisor who aligns with your requirements:

- **The Pro-Advisor Directory:** Search the online directory based on your location, industry, and desired area of expertise.
- **QuickBooks Support:** Contact QuickBooks support for personalized recommendations based on your specific needs and business type.
- **Word-of-Mouth Referrals:** Seek recommendations from colleagues, business partners, or your network of entrepreneurs who have positive experiences with Pro-Advisors.

Building a Strong Partnership:

Once you find a Pro-Advisor, effective communication and collaboration are key to maximizing their expertise:

- **Clearly Define Your Needs:** Clearly communicate your specific goals, challenges, and desired outcomes from the Pro-Advisor partnership.
- **Provide Accurate Information:** Ensure your Pro-Advisor has

access to accurate and up-to-date financial data for effective analysis and recommendations.

- **Ask Questions and Seek Clarification:** Don't hesitate to ask questions, seek clarification, and actively participate in the process to fully understand the Pro-Advisor's guidance.
- **Establish Communication Strategies:** Agree on regular communication channels, meeting schedules, and progress report frequency to maintain transparency and ensure smooth collaboration.

Empowering Your Financial Journey with Pro-Advisor Expertise

Partnering with a QuickBooks Pro-Advisor can be a game-changer for your financial management. Their specialized knowledge and personalized support can help you navigate complex financial situations, optimize your use of QuickBooks Online, and ultimately achieve your business goals.

Remember, a Pro-Advisor is not just a problem-solver; they are trusted partners who can empower you to make informed financial decisions, streamline your processes, and achieve long-term financial success. While there might be initial costs associated with engaging a Pro-Advisor, the long-term benefits of their expertise, efficiency gains, and potential tax and financial advantages often outweigh the investment. So, don't hesitate to seek their expertise when needed, and embark on a collaborative journey towards financial growth and prosperity.

42

Utilizing the QuickBooks Online Community

I
t's important to be part of an online community because even as QuickBooks Online is a powerful tool, even the most dedicated users encounter challenges or simply want to learn from others' experiences. Enter the vibrant QuickBooks Online community – a treasure trove of knowledge and support where you can connect with fellow users, experts, and Pro-Advisors.

This sub-chapter equips you with the knowledge to:

- **Navigate the Community Platform:** Discover the different sections and functionalities within the QuickBooks Online community to find the resources you need.
- **Ask Questions and Seek Answers:** Learn how to effectively pose questions, access existing solutions, and benefit from the collective wisdom of the community.
- **Share Knowledge and Support Others:** Contribute your own expertise, help fellow users, and build a sense of collaboration within the community.

Don't forget, the QuickBooks Online community is a valuable resource that can empower you to learn from others, troubleshoot challenges, and optimize your financial management journey. Let's delve into the specifics:

Exploring the Community Platform:

The QuickBooks Online community offers various resources to support your needs:

- **Q&A Forum:** This is the heart of the community, where you can post questions, browse existing discussions, and find solutions to common challenges.
- **Knowledge Base:** Access a vast library of articles, tutorials, and guides covering a wide range of QuickBooks Online functionalities and best practices.
- **Community Discussions:** Participate in ongoing conversations on specific topics, industry trends, and small business challenges, gaining valuable insights from diverse perspectives.

Asking the Right Questions:

To maximize the benefits of the community, learn how to effectively pose your questions:

- **Clearly Define Your Issue:** Provide a concise and specific description of your challenge or question, including relevant details and error messages if applicable.
- **Search Existing Discussions:** Before posting, utilize the search function to see if similar questions have already been addressed and answered within the community.

- **Categorize Your Question:** Select the appropriate category for your question to ensure it reaches the right audience and receives relevant responses.

Sharing Your Knowledge and Supporting Others:

The community thrives on collaboration. Here's how you can contribute:

- **Answer Questions:** Share your expertise and help fellow users by providing accurate and helpful solutions based on your experience.
- **Share Tips and Best Practices:** Contribute your own workflow optimizations, accounting strategies, and insights to benefit the broader community.
- **Up-vote Helpful Responses:** Acknowledge valuable contributions by up-voting helpful answers, making it easier for others to find the best solutions.

Building a Network of Support and Learning

The QuickBooks Online community is more than just a forum; it's a dynamic network of support and learning. By actively participating, you can:

- **Find Solutions to Challenges:** Gain valuable insights and troubleshooting tips from fellow users and experts to overcome any obstacle you might face.
- **Stay Updated on Best Practices:** Learn from the collective wisdom of the community, discover new features, and stay informed about the latest trends in financial management.
- **Build a Network of Support:** Connect with other small business

owners, entrepreneurs, and accounting professionals, fostering a sense of community and shared learning.

- **Forge Professional Connections:** The community can be a platform for building long-term professional relationships with like-minded individuals and potential collaborators, further expanding your network and accessing valuable resources.

Keep in mind, the QuickBooks Online community is a powerful resource at your fingertips. Utilize it to ask questions, share your knowledge, and build a network of support that empowers you to navigate your financial management journey with confidence and success. So, dive into the community, connect with others, and embark on a collaborative learning experience that will benefit your business in the long run.

X

QuickBooks Online Best Practices and Tips

43

Developing a Bookkeeping Routine

Maintaining accurate and organized financial records is the cornerstone of any successful business. QuickBooks Online provides powerful tools to simplify this process, but it's the consistent application of good bookkeeping practices that truly unlocks its potential.

Defining Your Bookkeeping Goals:

Before diving into the routine, understand the core objectives of bookkeeping:

- **Accurate Financial Reporting:** Track your income, expenses, and overall financial health to gain valuable insights into your business's performance. This allows you to identify trends, analyze profitability, and make data-driven decisions.
- **Tax Compliance:** Maintain organized records for tax preparation and ensure adherence to relevant regulations. Accurate bookkeeping minimizes the risk of errors and penalties during tax season.
- **Informed Decision-Making:** Utilize financial data to make

strategic business decisions, identify areas for improvement, and optimize your financial strategies. Bookkeeping provides a clear picture of your financial situation, empowering you to allocate resources effectively and make informed choices for growth.

Establishing a Structured Routine:

Consistency is key to effective bookkeeping. Here's how to build a routine that works for you:

- **Schedule Regular Entry Times:** Dedicate specific days or times each week to record transactions, categorize expenses, and reconcile accounts. This creates a consistent workflow and prevents tasks from piling up.
- **Automate Recurring Tasks:** Leverage QuickBooks Online's automation features to automatically record recurring transactions like rent, subscriptions, or loan payments. This saves time and minimizes manual data entry errors.
- **Set Realistic Deadlines:** Establish achievable deadlines for completing bookkeeping tasks, ensuring you stay on top of your financial data. Deadlines provide accountability and prevent procrastination.

Real-Life Example: Imagine a small bakery owner who receives daily cash register receipts. They dedicate an hour every Tuesday afternoon to record these transactions in QuickBooks Online, categorize them as sales, and reconcile their bank account to ensure accuracy. This routine ensures timely financial record keeping and avoids potential discrepancies, allowing the owner to monitor daily sales performance and cash flow.

Leveraging QuickBooks Online Features:

QuickBooks Online offers a wealth of features to streamline your bookkeeping process:

- **Bank Feeds:** Connect your bank accounts to automatically download transactions, saving time and reducing manual data entry. This eliminates the need for manually entering each transaction, minimizing errors and ensuring accuracy.
- **Smart Receipt Capture:** Utilize the mobile app to capture receipts and automatically categorize expenses, eliminating the need for manual data entry. This simplifies expense tracking and streamlines the categorization process.
- **Reporting Tools:** Generate financial reports like Profit and Loss statements and Balance Sheets to gain insights into your business's financial performance. These reports provide a comprehensive overview of your income, expenses, assets, and liabilities, enabling you to track profitability, identify trends, and make informed financial decisions.
- **Accounts Receivable and Accounts Payable Aging Reports:** These reports provide a detailed breakdown of outstanding invoices and bills, allowing you to proactively manage your cash flow and avoid overdue payments. By monitoring aging reports, you can identify late payments, prioritize collections, and ensure timely payments to vendors.

Building a Foundation for Financial Growth

Developing a consistent bookkeeping routine with QuickBooks Online is an investment in your business's future. By following these steps, you'll gain:

- **Improved Financial Visibility:** Track your income, expenses, and overall financial health with clarity and accuracy. You'll have a clear understanding of your financial position, enabling you to make informed decisions and identify areas for improvement.
- **Enhanced Efficiency:** Automate tasks, reduce manual data entry, and free up valuable time for other business activities. This allows you to focus on core business operations and strategic initiatives.
- **Confident Decision-Making:** Utilize financial data to make informed business decisions, identify growth opportunities, and achieve your financial goals. With accurate and readily available financial information, you can make strategic choices that drive business success.

Remember, a well-defined bookkeeping routine is not just a chore; it's a foundation for financial growth and stability. By consistently utilizing QuickBooks Online's features and maintaining accurate records, you empower yourself to navigate the financial landscape of your business with confidence and make informed decisions that propel your success. So, embrace the power of routine, leverage technology, and build a strong financial foundation for your business with QuickBooks Online.

44

Securing Your Financial Data

I n today's digital world, safeguarding your financial information is paramount. QuickBooks Online prioritizes data security, but proactive measures on your end further strengthen this protection.

Mind you, a layered approach to security maximizes the protection of your financial data in QuickBooks Online. Let's delve into the specifics:

QuickBooks Online's Security Infrastructure:

QuickBooks Online employs a multi-layered security approach, including:

- **Advanced Encryption:** Data is encrypted using industry-standard AES 256 encryption, the same level used by leading financial institutions, ensuring its protection even in the unlikely event of a breach.
- **Secure Logins:** Password-protected logins with two-factor authentication add an extra layer of security, requiring both a password and a unique code sent to your phone or email for access.

- **Firewall Protection:** Robust firewalls safeguard QuickBooks Online servers, filtering incoming and outgoing traffic to prevent unauthorized access.

- **Automatic Backups:** QuickBooks Online automatically backs up your data regularly, ensuring its safety even in case of hardware failures or natural disasters.

Best Practices for Enhanced Security:

While QuickBooks Online provides a strong foundation, consider these additional measures:

- **Create Strong Passwords:** Utilize complex passwords with a combination of uppercase and lowercase letters, numbers, and symbols. Avoid using easily guessable information like birthdays or names.

- **Enable Two-Factor Authentication:** This adds an extra layer of security by requiring a unique code sent to your phone or email in addition to your password.

- **Grant User Access Wisely:** Only grant access to your QuickBooks Online account to authorized individuals and assign appropriate permission levels based on their specific needs. This ensures that users can only access the information they require for their specific tasks.

- **Monitor User Activity:** Regularly review user activity logs to identify any suspicious behavior or unauthorized access attempts. This allows you to detect potential breaches early on.

- **Stay Updated:** Keep your computer and browser software updated with the latest security patches to minimize vulnerabilities. Outdated software can contain security gaps that cybercriminals can exploit.

Real-Life Example:
Imagine a small clothing boutique owner using QuickBooks Online. They implement strong password practices with a combination of uppercase and lowercase letters, numbers, and symbols. They also enable two-factor authentication and only grant their assistant access to enter sales transactions. Additionally, they regularly review user activity logs and update their software to ensure optimal security. These proactive measures significantly reduce the risk of unauthorized access to their sensitive financial data.

Maintaining Vigilance: Ongoing Security Measures

Data security is an ongoing process. Here are additional tips for long-term protection:

- **Beware of Phishing Attempts:** Be cautious of suspicious emails or websites requesting your login credentials or financial information. QuickBooks Online will never ask for sensitive information via email. Common phishing attempts targeting small businesses include:
- **Fake Invoices:** Emails disguised as invoices from legitimate vendors, often containing malicious attachments or links that can steal your login information.
- **Urgent Requests:** Emails claiming urgent financial issues or overdue payments, pressuring you to click on links or provide sensitive information without proper verification.
- **Software Updates:** Emails posing as official software updates from QuickBooks, containing malware or phishing links disguised as download buttons.
- **Use a Secure Internet Connection:** Avoid accessing your Quick-

Books Online account on public Wi-Fi networks, as they are less secure than private connections. Public Wi-Fi networks can be easily compromised, potentially exposing your data to eavesdropping.

- **Stay Informed:** Keep yourself updated on the latest cybersecurity threats and best practices to adapt your security measures accordingly. Resources like the QuickBooks Online Security Center provide valuable information and updates on emerging threats and how to protect yourself.

Building a Secure Financial Future

By understanding QuickBooks Online's security features, implementing best practices, and remaining vigilant, you create a robust shield for your financial data. Remember, data security is a shared responsibility. By taking these proactive steps, you empower yourself to manage your finances with confidence and minimize the risk of cyber threats, ensuring the long-term security of your financial information within QuickBooks Online. So, prioritize data security, stay informed, and build a secure foundation for your financial future.

45

Mobile App and Remote Access Features

I n today's digital age, staying connected to your finances is no longer a luxury, but a necessity. QuickBooks Online empowers you to manage your financial data anytime, anywhere, thanks to its robust mobile app and remote access features.

Remember, the ability to manage your finances remotely is a game-changer for modern businesses. Let's unlock the potential of these features:

The Power of the QuickBooks Online Mobile App:

The QuickBooks Online mobile app is your pocket-sized financial companion, offering a range of functionalities that empower you to manage your finances on the go:

- **Real-Time Financial Tracking:** Monitor your income, expenses, and cash flow in real-time, providing instant insights into your financial health. This allows you to make informed decisions based on up-to-date financial data, even when you're away from your computer.

- **Effortless Expense Management:** Capture and categorize receipts on the go using your phone's camera, eliminating manual data entry and ensuring accurate expense tracking. This saves you time and minimizes the risk of errors associated with manual data entry.

- **Streamlined Invoicing:** Create and send invoices to customers directly from your mobile device, accelerating the billing process and improving cash flow. This eliminates the need to wait until you're back at your office computer to send invoices, potentially leading to faster payments.

- **Mobile Payments:** Accept credit card payments through the app, offering your customers convenient payment options and boosting your cash flow efficiency. This provides greater flexibility for your customers and allows you to receive payments more quickly.

- **Simplified Banking:** Reconcile your bank statements and track transactions directly within the app, saving time and simplifying bank account management. This eliminates the need to switch between different platforms and streamlines your bank reconciliation process.

- **Mileage Tracking:** Track your business mileage automatically or manually, maximizing tax deductions and simplifying expense reporting. This automates a tedious task and ensures accurate mileage records for tax purposes.

- **Inventory Management:** Add, edit, and track inventory levels directly from the app, ensuring accurate stock control and efficient order management. This provides real-time insights into your inventory levels and allows you to make informed decisions regarding restocking.

- **Bill Pay:** Pay bills directly through the app, streamlining your accounts payable process and improving cash flow management.

This eliminates the need for manual check writing and simplifies bill payments, saving you time and effort.

Real-Life Example:

Imagine a landscaper working on a client's property. They can use the mobile app to capture receipts for plants and materials purchased, create and send an invoice to the client on the spot, and even track their mileage throughout the day. This eliminates the need for manual record keeping and ensures accurate financial data, even when they are away from their office.

Remote Access: Unlocking Flexibility

QuickBooks Online goes beyond the mobile app, allowing you to access your financial data from any internet-connected device:

- **Remote Desktop Access:** Utilize remote desktop software to access your primary computer where QuickBooks Online is installed, enabling you to work on your financial data from anywhere. This provides the same functionality as if you were working directly on your office computer, regardless of your location.
- **Cloud-Based Accessibility:** Since QuickBooks Online is cloud-based, you can directly access your data through a web browser on any device, eliminating the need for remote desktop software. This offers even greater flexibility and accessibility, allowing you to work from any device with an internet connection.

Real-Life Example:

A small business owner needs to review a financial report while traveling. They can easily access their QuickBooks Online account through a web browser on their laptop at the airport, ensuring they can stay on top of their finances even when away from their office. This allows them to make timely decisions and address any urgent financial matters remotely.

Maximizing Efficiency and Convenience:

The combined power of the mobile app and remote access offers numerous benefits that can significantly enhance your financial management:

- **Increased Productivity:** Manage your finances on the go, saving time and allowing you to be more productive, regardless of your location. This frees you from being tied to your office computer and allows you to work more efficiently.
- **Enhanced Flexibility:** Work from anywhere with an internet connection, offering greater flexibility and adapting to your dynamic business needs. This allows you to manage your finances even when you are traveling, working remotely, or simply away from the office for any reason.
- **Improved Collaboration:** Share financial data with your team members or accountant remotely, facilitating collaboration and streamlining workflows. This allows for real-time collaboration on financial tasks and improves communication within your team.

Unlocking Financial Freedom

QuickBooks Online's mobile app and remote access features revolutionize how you manage your finances. By leveraging these functionalities, you gain the freedom to access your financial data anytime, anywhere, empowering you to make informed decisions, improve efficiency, and ultimately achieve greater financial success. So, embrace the mobility and flexibility offered by these features, and unlock a new era of financial freedom for your business.

Bonus Chapter: QuickBooks Online 2024 Cheat Sheet

Life gets busy, and sometimes you just need a quick refresher on where to find things or how to do a specific task. That's where this guide comes in. We'll cover essential concepts, common tasks with mini-guides, and even some handy resources to keep you on top of your game.

Accounting Terms at a Glance:

Ever come across a term in QuickBooks Online that leaves you scratching your head? Don't worry, accounting can have its own language. This quick reference list will help you decode some of the most common ones you'll encounter:

- **Accounts Payable:** Money you owe to vendors for goods or services received (think "bills to be paid").
- **Accounts Receivable:** Money owed to you by customers for goods or services you've provided (think "invoices waiting to be collected").
- **Assets:** Resources your business owns that have value (like cash, equipment, or inventory).
- **Debits & Credits:** These aren't insults in the accounting world! They represent opposite sides of a transaction – debits increase expenses or assets and decrease liabilities or equity, while credits do the opposite.

- **Equity:** The owner's claim on the business's assets after liabilities are subtracted (basically, what's truly yours after all the bills are paid).
- **Liabilities:** Debts your business owes, like loans or unpaid taxes.
- **Profit & Loss (P&L):** A report summarizing your business's income and expenses over a period, showing your net profit or loss.

QBO Tasks in a Flash:

Need a quick reminder on how to tackle some essential tasks in QuickBooks Online? Here are mini-guides to get you going:

Creating an Invoice:

1. Click on "Sales" and then "Create Invoice."
2. Select the customer you're billing.
3. Add your products or services, including quantities and prices.
4. Choose a due date and any custom message for the customer.
5. Click "Save and Send" to email the invoice directly.

Running a Profit & Loss Report:

1. Go to "Reports" and then "Profit and Loss."
2. Select the date range you want to see (e.g., this month, last quarter).
3. You can customize the report further by clicking on the wrench icon and adjusting filters or columns.

Reconciling a Bank Account:

1. Click on "Banking" and then "Reconcile."
2. Select the bank account you want to reconcile.
3. Match up your bank statement transactions with the ones showing in QuickBooks Online.

4. Click "Mark as Reconciled" when all transactions are matched.

Remember, these are just quick snapshots. If you need a more detailed walkthrough, refer back to the relevant chapters in this guide for step-by-step instructions.

Sometimes, the most useful bits are the hidden gems within the software. Here are a few worth remembering:

- **The Search Bar:** It's your time-saving friend! Instead of clicking through multiple menus, type in what you need (e.g., "create bill," "customer statement") in the search bar at the top. QuickBooks Online takes you there instantly.
- **Customizable Reports:** Most financial reports can be tweaked and filtered to show exactly what you need. Click on that little wrench icon on report screens to play around– see if sales by product, customer balances, or other customized views make the numbers more meaningful.
- **"Help" Tab:** When all else fails, that tiny "Help" tab in the top right corner of QuickBooks Online is your lifeline. Get live chat assistance (depending on your subscription), search for answers, or even get connected with a QuickBooks Online expert if you need a deeper dive.

Mastering the Lingo:

Accounting vocabulary can feel overwhelming, so here are a few extra terms that pop up often in QuickBooks Online and are great to know:

- **Chart of Accounts:** The backbone of organizing your finances – it's a list of all your income, expense, asset, and liability accounts.

- **General Ledger:** Where every single transaction (invoice, bill, expense, etc.) your business makes gets recorded for all eternity. Consider this the master record behind your financial reports.
- **Receipt Capture:** This handy feature in the QuickBooks Online mobile app lets you snap photos of paper receipts and have them automatically uploaded, categorizing the expenses for you.
- **Accrual vs. Cash Basis Accounting:** This determines when income & expenses are actually recognized in your books. Accrual is when it's *earned* or *incurred*, cash basis is simply when the money flows in or out of your bank account. QuickBooks Online lets you choose!

Mobile App Power-Ups:

QuickBooks Online on your phone or tablet isn't just a mini version of the desktop experience – it unlocks some serious on-the-go convenience:

- **Create & Send on the Spot:** Need to invoice a customer right after a job is done? Do it right there, directly from the app. No more forgotten notes to input later!
- **Expense Tracking on the Go:** Say goodbye to a shoebox full of receipts. Use the app's "Receipt Capture" to photograph, record and categorize those expenses the moment they're incurred.
- **Instant Dashboard Views:** How's the business doing at a glance? The mobile app's dashboard gives a quick snapshot of key numbers – perfect for when you have a spare moment to check in.

Words of Wisdom

Finally, always remember these golden rules when using QuickBooks Online:

- **Consistency is Key:** The more regularly you enter your transactions, the better your reports and insights will be. It's a little bit every day, not a frantic catch-up session at the end of the month.
- **Backups are Your Best Friend:** QuickBooks Online backs things up automatically, but it's smart to also export your data regularly as extra insurance. You never know when you might need a snapshot of the past!
- **Explore as You Go:** QuickBooks Online has so much to offer. Don't be afraid to click around and experiment – that's how you'll find features that truly change the way you manage your business finances.

Bonus Chapter: QuickBooks Desktop Pro 2024 Shortcuts List

Let's face it, navigating software with just a mouse can feel like taking the scenic route when you just want to get there fast. That's where keyboard shortcuts come in – they're like magic spells that whisk you straight to the functions you use most often in QuickBooks Online. This list will become your secret weapon for mastering the software with lightning speed!

Navigation Shortcuts:
These shortcuts will get you around QuickBooks Online like a seasoned pro:

- **Home:** Go back to the QuickBooks Online home screen.
- **Ctrl + Tab:** Switch between open tabs.
- **Ctrl + F:** Open the search bar to find anything quickly (invoices, customers, reports, etc.).
- **Up/Down Arrows:** Navigate through lists and menus.
- **Enter:** Select the highlighted option.
- **Esc:** Close out of any open windows or menus.

Creating Transactions:
Need to whip up an invoice or record an expense in a flash? These shortcuts are your ticket:

- **Ctrl + N:** Create a new invoice.
- **Ctrl + P:** Create a new purchase order.
- **Ctrl + B:** Create a new bill.
- **Ctrl + E:** Create a new expense.
- **Tab:** Move between fields when creating a transaction.

Editing Transactions:

Let's say you need to make a quick change to an invoice. No problem!

- **Double-click:** This opens the highlighted transaction for editing (works in most lists and reports).
- **F2:** Edit the name of a customer, vendor, or account.
- **Ctrl + Delete:** Delete a transaction (be careful with this one!).

Action Shortcuts:

These shortcuts take common actions without needing to navigate through menus:

- **Ctrl + S:** Save the current transaction or report.
- **Ctrl + P:** Print the current transaction or report.
- **Ctrl + Shft + S:** Send the current invoice or form directly to your customer.

Advanced User Shortcuts:

Feeling comfortable and want to take it to the next level? These shortcuts are for you:

- **Ctrl + . (period):** Mark a transaction as paid (great for speeding through your bank reconciliation).
- **Ctrl + , (comma):** Mark a transaction as to be emailed (helpful for sending out a batch of invoices at once).

- **Ctrl + Shft + H:** Open the Chart of Accounts (the heart of your financial organization!).

Date Shortcuts

Working with dates is a constant in accounting. Make it quick and easy with these:

- **T:** Automatically enters today's date.
- **Y:** Automatically enters yesterday's date.
- **+ :** Moves forward one day from the current date in a date field.
- **- :** Moves backward one day from the current date in a date field.
- **M** : Jumps to the first day of the current month.

Reporting Shortcuts

Shortcuts aren't just for creating transactions – they speed up report viewing too!

- **Ctrl + Alt + R:** Opens your list of memorized reports (those reports you have custom-saved to revisit frequently).
- **F3:** Opens the "Customize Report" window to tweak filters and columns.
- **Left/Right Arrows:** When viewing a report, move between columns for easier scanning.

Shortcut ProTips

- **Windows vs. Mac:** Most of these shortcuts use the "Ctrl" key for Windows users. If you're on a Mac, substitute the "Ctrl" key with the "Command" key.
- **Conflicting Shortcuts:** Some of these shortcuts might mirror

your browser's shortcuts (like Ctrl + P for print). Browser shortcuts will usually override QuickBooks Online ones.

Remembering It All:

Don't worry about memorizing every shortcut overnight! Here are a few tips:

- **QuickBooks Online Built-in Cheat Sheet:** Did you know there's a keyboard shortcut list readily available within the software itself? Press **Ctrl + Alt + ?** to bring it up anytime.
- **Practice Makes Perfect:** The more you use these shortcuts, the more ingrained they'll become in your muscle memory.
- **Focus on the Most Used:** Start by learning the shortcuts you use most often, and gradually add more to your repertoire.

By incorporating these keyboard shortcuts into your QuickBooks Online routine, you'll be amazed at how much faster and more efficient you become. So unleash your inner keyboard ninja and conquer your accounting tasks in record time!

Bonus Chapter: Free Consultation Services

Sometimes, even with a fantastic guide (and believe me, this one is great!), and super user-friendly software like QuickBooks Online, you just need a real person to help you through a specific snag or just to get that extra boost of confidence. That's where free consultations and resources come in, and guess what? There are more options than you might think!

Why Take Advantage of a Free Consultation?

Let's be real, sometimes accounting, no matter how streamlined the software, makes you want to pull your hair out. Free consultation offer you a lifeline, and there are several good reasons to make use of them:

- **Personalized Help:** Every business is unique. A consultant can look at your *specific* financials and business setup and offer advice tailored to you – something no guidebook can completely replicate.
- **Unblock Those Roadblocks:** Stuck figuring out that weird tax situation? Can't make a report show the data you need? Consultants are great at getting you unstuck quickly.
- **Expert Insights:** Beyond specific questions, a consultation can expose you to features in QuickBooks Online or accounting best practices you didn't even know about, which can supercharge your efficiency.
- **Peace of Mind:** Feeling uncertain and anxious about your books isn't good for anyone! Sometimes all it takes is chatting with a

reassuring expert who can confirm you're doing things right, or give you a gentle course correction.

To get access to free consultation, contact the author at robert-wallen24@gmail.com or scan the QR code

Bonus Chapter: QuickBooks Learning Tracker

How to Use the QuickBooks Learning Tracker

Congratulations on taking charge of your business finances with QuickBooks Online! But with any new software, there's a learning curve. That's where the QuickBooks Learning Tracker, included in this book, comes in.

Think of it as your personalized roadmap to QuickBooks Online mastery. It's a place to track your progress, record those "aha!" moments, and identify areas where you might want to spend a little extra practice time.

Breaking Down the Tracker:

The tracker is divided into four sections to help you monitor your learning journey:

- **Date/Chapter:** Here, you'll note the date you tackled a particular chapter in this guide and match it to the corresponding chapter number.
- **What You Learnt:** This is your chance to jot down the key takeaways from each chapter. Did you discover a cool new feature? Learn a shortcut that will save you time? Write it all down here!
- **Practice Experience:** This is where things get real. After reading a chapter, put your newfound knowledge into action! Practice what

you learned in QuickBooks Online. Did everything go smoothly? Did you encounter any roadblocks? Note your experience here.

- **Remarks:** This is your designated space for anything else that comes to mind. Maybe a question popped up that you want to research later, or an idea for how you can apply what you learned to your specific business. Use this section to personalize your learning journey.

Why Use the Tracker?

Filling out this tracker might seem optional, but trust me, it's a powerful tool for several reasons:

- **Solidifying Your Knowledge:** The act of writing things down is a fantastic way to solidify what you've learned.
- **Identifying Gaps:** If you find yourself consistently struggling with a particular concept in the "Practice Experience" section, you'll know to revisit that chapter or explore the resources mentioned in the book for further guidance.
- **Tracking Your Progress:** There's something super motivating about seeing those completed sections in your tracker. It's a visual reminder of how far you've come on your QuickBooks Online journey!
- **Building Confidence:** As you fill in your tracker, you'll watch your knowledge and confidence with QuickBooks Online grow. That "aha!" moment when you finally master a new feature is an awesome feeling!

Tips for Using the Tracker Effectively

- **Don't Be Intimidated:** There's no right or wrong way to use the tracker. It's yours to personalize!

- **Be Honest:** The tracker is for your own benefit. If something confused you, write it down! That way you can revisit it later or ask for help.
- **Keep it Going:** Try to fill out the tracker as you progress through the book. The sooner you write things down, the easier it will be to remember the details.
- **Make it Fun:** Who says learning can't be fun? Decorate your tracker, use different colored pens – anything to keep yourself engaged.

The QuickBooks Learning Tracker is your secret weapon for conquering QuickBooks Online. Use it, personalize it, and watch your accounting skills flourish!

quickbooks learning tracker

DATE/CHAPTER	WHAT YOU LEARNT	PRACTICE EXPERIENCE	REMARK

IMPORTANT NOTE

quickbooks learning tracker

DATE/CHAPTER	WHAT YOU LEARNT	PRACTICE EXPERIENCE	REMARK

IMPORTANT NOTE

quickbooks learning tracker

DATE/CHAPTER	WHAT YOU LEARNT	PRACTICE EXPERIENCE	REMARK

IMPORTANT NOTE

quickbooks
learning
tracker

DATE/CHAPTER	WHAT YOU LEARNT	PRACTICE EXPERIENCE	REMARK

IMPORTANT NOTE

quickbooks learning tracker

DATE/CHAPTER	WHAT YOU LEARNT	PRACTICE EXPERIENCE	REMARK

IMPORTANT NOTE

quickbooks learning tracker

DATE/CHAPTER	WHAT YOU LEARNT	PRACTICE EXPERIENCE	REMARK

IMPORTANT NOTE

quickbooks learning tracker

DATE/CHAPTER	WHAT YOU LEARNT	PRACTICE EXPERIENCE	REMARK

IMPORTANT NOTE

quickbooks learning tracker

DATE/CHAPTER	WHAT YOU LEARNT	PRACTICE EXPERIENCE	REMARK

IMPORTANT NOTE

Made in United States
Orlando, FL
24 September 2024

51910537R00163